LEADERSHIP
TREASURE

*Led with courage
and compassion.*

Jill White

LEADERSHIP
TREASURE

25 BITS OF GOLD
DISCOVERED
FROM 25 YEARS
AS A CEO

JEFF WHITEHORN

Whitehorn Press

For information:

Whitehorn Press

9442 Highwood Hill Road, Brentwood, TN 37027
email: info@jeffwhitehorn.com, or visit: www.jeffwhitehorn.com

Production and creative:
Epiphany Creative Services LLC

Library of Congress Cataloging-in-Publication Data
Library of Congress Control Number: 2021901767

FIRST EDITION
Jeff Whitehorn – 1st ed.
TITLE: LeadershipTreasure:
25 Bits of Gold Discovered From 25 Years as a CEO
p. cm.

Print ISBN: 978-1-7362377-0-0
eBook ISBN: 978-1-7362377-1-7

BUS071000 BUSINESS & ECONOMICS / Leadership

Printed in the United States of America

Distributed by Whitehorn Press
14   10 9 8 7 6 5 4 3 2 1

Contents

For Jennifer,
the love of my life and my best friend.
For Ashleigh and Emily,
our beautiful daughters whom I love.

Introduction

Whoever first said "I wish I knew then what I know now" was a genius. Wouldn't you agree? I've thought about that statement many times as I've looked back on my twenty-five-year career as a CEO. I'm certain that I would have been a better leader if only I would have known what I didn't know. Experience is priceless, and it should be shared with others.

I have always loved learning from other leaders, whether reading their books, attending their seminars, or listening to their keynote speeches. My goal was to always find a few "bits of gold" from all the material that was presented in their educational events or written in their books. Too many ideas will sometimes spin your wheels but get you nowhere. However, I knew that if I could focus on implementing just two or three of the most helpful tips given by proven leaders, then I would be a better leader. I soon called these tips "leadership treasure."

I picked up quite a few bits of gold as a leader myself, and I want to share them with you. I learned the most from real-life leaders, not from listening to entertaining, professional presenters with slick presentations discussing nothing more than basic Leadership 101 principles. Plus, the vast majority of them had never led and managed people "in the real world." I understand the challenges, pressures, and hardships that confront leaders because I personally experienced it "in the real world."

I began my leadership journey in 1988 at Charter Lake Hospital, a small hospital in Macon, Georgia, as an assistant administrator. I retired twenty-nine years later in 2017 at age fifty-five as CEO of TriStar Summit Medical Center, a large hospital in Hermitage, Tennessee, located just outside Nashville. I had the wonderful opportunity to lead Summit for fourteen years. I served as CEO at several other hospitals along my leadership journey before arriving at Summit. I was a "lifer" with HCA Healthcare, working twenty-five years with this outstanding company. God blessed me with the opportunity to do what I loved most—lead others in order to help patients improve and get well. Today, I'm the founder of Whitehorn Coaching & Consulting, and I coach other leaders to grow and develop their leadership skills.

If you want to discover some leadership treasure in order to become a better leader, then this book is for you. If you want short, get-to-the-point chapters without lots of needless fluff, then this book is for you. If you want to learn from someone who sat in your chair as a leader for twenty-nine years, then this book is for you. My goal is to help you become a better leader.

Are you ready to discover some leadership treasure? If so, then let's go!

Got Hustle?

"Without hustle, talent will only carry you so far."
— Gary Vaynerchuk, entrepreneur

I was sitting at the table with some of my closest friends at our annual high school sports banquet. It was 1977. Most of us wore sport coats with wide lapels, clip-on ties, and shoes from Sears. I would have worn my silky Qiana shirt displaying a sunset over the lake, along with my white leisure suit and blue platform shoes, but Mom nixed that idea. Disco was in, and the soundtrack of *Saturday Night Fever* was *the* eight-track tape that you had to own to be considered cool.

Coaches announced and presented the awards for football. Oh, how I love the game of football. A close friend of mine was awarded Most Valuable Player (MVP). I was elated for him! He was talented and worked hard. He had a really good year and deserved the MVP award.

The presentation of basketball awards was up next. I loved our basketball team. The teamwork, camaraderie, and success were invigorating. We always had a good team. I was thrilled when another of my closest friends was named MVP of our team! He was a tireless worker who both practiced hard and played hard. Without a doubt, he was a true MVP.

A new award was being given that year, one that our team voted on. Privately, I felt that I had a shot at this award but didn't want to get my hopes up. I always gave it everything I had playing ball, never leaving anything in the tank. I wasn't tall, and I didn't score very often, but I had an incredible desire to win. It was pure ecstasy to make an assist to a teammate who scored or to steal the ball while playing defense. I tried to be the guy that you hated to see guard you. I would do everything I could to harass you, to stay so close to you without fouling, and to get into your head. I was a pest to the man I covered, and I loved it. I might not have been the MVP, but there was a role for everyone on the team. Mine was to dish the ball to my teammates, play defense, and to outhustle our competition.

And the Winner Is . . .

The coach said a few nice things about the yet-unnamed recipient of the award. It sounded like me, but I didn't want to get my hopes up. It felt like it took forever for him to say the name. I was nervous—sweaty palms, slightly short of breath.

Then the coach finally announced the winner of the Hustle Award—and it was me. I was so excited, so honored. I always gave it my all, and my teammates had noticed. It was an incredible feeling that night, one I will never forget. Little did I know the impact that it would have on my life—a small, inexpensive, plastic trophy called the Hustle Award. However, it had my name engraved on it. I displayed it in every office I occupied until I retired. It remains visible in my home office to this day.

As weird as it may sound, I've always viewed the Hustle Award as symbolic of my professional life. I realized early on that I'm not the smartest of the group. Don't get me wrong, I was an OK student in college. Tried my hardest to be a straight-A student but came up a little short at times. Same thing as an executive—in the zone but not quite as talented as some of the others.

However, I knew that if I wanted to win, I would have to outhustle others. As CEO, I had to outhustle our competitors in order to win in the marketplace. I loved competing, and I loved to win—and to win big. The way I looked at it, I had more hustle than talent. This was my strength, and I used it as my competitive advantage. Therefore, I committed to myself that no one would outhustle me if I could help it, ever.

Do You Hustle or Rely on Talent?

I loved hiring people who hustled. I always looked for talent, but I hired more people based on hustle. I loved employees who had the will to win, the will to overcome obstacles, and the will to prove that they deserved the job. You could hear the passion in their voices as they told stories of what they had overcome to achieve success, whether in the work setting or in their personal lives. Those were the winners I wanted on our team. Maybe this was because of my inward reflection. I yearned to win, but I knew I had to hustle to do so. I simply loved those who hustled and achieved great things in their careers because they gave it their all. I was inspired by them.

The desire and strength to hustle comes from within. You can't hope for it. You can't wish for it. It's a commitment that you make with yourself. It's the action you take in order to be the very best you can be. To me, someone who hustles possesses the following characteristics:

H - Hunger to win and to win big
U - Unselfish
S - Stays focused
T - Team player
L - Loves to overachieve
E - Enthusiastic

One Question, Two Words

Do you possess hustle or talent, or both? Both can be developed and improved, but it's up to you to make it happen. Hustle is an inward, unquenchable drive to succeed. It's getting up every day, looking at yourself in the mirror, and committing to hustle the entire day, whether at work or in life. Those who hustle seem to always find a way to win. They don't always get the credit they deserve, but they are critical players on the team. You will overachieve with them and underachieve without them. Talent makes you good, but talent with hustle makes you great.

One question, two words: Got hustle?

Now, what about you?

1. What metaphor symbolizes your inner desire to be a great leader?
2. How do you display this desire every day to your team?

Love Your Job

"To be successful, the first thing to do
is fall in love with your work."
— Sister Mary Lauretta,
former high school science teacher

What am I going to do? I stared out the window of our CPA firm's downtown office. It was a cold, foggy, and rainy November morning in Nashville, Tennessee, in 1985. I was sitting in a row of shared cubicles designated for traveling auditors. I happened to be in the office that day, which was a rarity. I couldn't concentrate on the spreadsheet on the desk in front of me. My mechanical pencils and ten-key calculator were untouched. My old leather audit bag was on the floor beside me. Other than a mailbox with my name on it, I had nothing else to call my own in that office.

It was deathly quiet—everyone was working but no one was talking. *What am I doing here? I love to talk! Does anyone want to talk about the football game last night? Does anyone notice this wild and crazy new paisley tie I'm wearing? You mean, I polished my black wing-tip shoes for this? Am I really talking to myself again?* Deep down, I knew the accounting profession wasn't for me. I continued staring out the window, pondering what job I could do that I would love.

I was honored to work as a staff accountant at KPMG, a large CPA firm. It was my first job straight out of college. Public accounting was the career I had chosen. I had a total of three suits, five shirts, and five ties—man, I looked good! In the beginning, my goal was to become a partner in the CPA firm someday. The desire for achieving that goal, however, diminished daily. After about a year and a half, I knew I needed to do something else. The problem: *What will I do?*

I Think I Need an MBA

My wife, Jennifer, and I were newlyweds. We had only been married for about three months. Jennifer is my best friend and greatest encourager. With her support, I decided to go back to school to get my MBA. So much was being touted about the importance of an MBA in the mid-'80s and how it could help your career. In my mind, the letters CPA and MBA after my name would surely position me well for whatever I was going to do. Of course, the question "What am I going to do?" had to be answered first.

Then—bam!—I figured it out. The summer between my first and second year of graduate school at the University of Alabama, I worked as an intern at Lloyd Noland Hospital in Birmingham. I was fascinated by the operational challenges the hospital faced, the need for a committed team, and the mission of helping others. I observed that the CEO was accountable for the results of the hospital, both good and bad. For me, being a hospital CEO combined business skills with a personal mission: helping others. *I can do this*, I thought. *Yes, this is what I want to do!* I was so jazzed—I had finally answered the question: "What am I going to do?" I was going to be a hospital CEO.

Upon graduation, and for the next twenty-nine years, I served as a hospital administrator. I moved from assistant administrator to COO, and from COO to CEO. The job far exceeded my expectations as I served as a CEO for twenty-five years. I never looked back. It fulfilled my wildest dreams. Simply stated, I absolutely loved my job!

The Foundation of Great Leadership

Great leaders truly love their jobs. I mean, really love them. A passion for what you do must burn in your heart in order to be an extraordinary leader. Sure, there will be days when you drive home and you say to yourself, "I'm not paid nearly enough for going through what I had to endure today." Everyone has those days—it's just a part of work. However, I'm talking about the other 95 percent of the days when you drive home and you know you made a difference. You contributed in some way that either helped others or that moved your organization forward. You added value.

Loving your job is the foundation of great leadership. Employees are more apt to follow leaders who love their jobs and care about them as staff. It's the basis for motivating others, achieving company goals, and delivering a product or service that makes you proud. In fact, it's really not just a job to you—it's your opportunity to do what you love.

Finding Your Sweet Spot

I challenge you to find a job you love, one that you know was meant for you. In other words, find your sweet spot. Find the job that is the right fit for you. Your sweet spot is the job that checks off all the boxes you identified that will make you happy.

Serving as CEO for TriStar Summit Medical Center was my sweet spot. I loved my job, and it fulfilled my dream for fourteen years. It challenged me like none other. I loved our team. I loved our physicians. I loved our mission of helping others. I'm convinced that God led me to Summit. It provided the gratification that I needed and wanted in my professional career. It also allowed Jennifer, my wonderful and supportive wife, and me to not have to relocate our family to another city in order to advance within the company. That was our goal. That's not everyone's goal, and that's OK. For us, however, it was very important. My job at Summit was my sweet spot.

What Can You Do to Love Your Job?

Do you love your job? If not, what can you do to elevate what you do in order to love your job?

1. **Find meaning.** Look at how your job adds value to your organization. Everyone has a role in order to achieve a goal. Therefore, what you do matters.
2. **Learn something new.** Challenge yourself to volunteer to take on something that you haven't done before.
3. **Ask for additional duties.** Let your boss know that you want to take on more. Ask your boss what they can delegate to you in order to help them. Go the extra

mile.

4. **Practice gratitude.** Be thankful that you have been given the opportunity to have your job. Remember, there is always a line of folks who want your job.

5. **Create laughter and fun.** Add some fun and zest into your work and with those around you. Smile and laugh more!

On a scale of 1 to 10, how satisfied are you with your job? Loving your job maximizes your happiness both at work and at home.

Now, what about you?

1. What parts of your job do you love the most? Why?
2. What can you do to grow to love your job more?

3

Family First—Always

"If you want to change the world,
go home and love your family."
— Mother Teresa,
nun and missionary

Y ou are considered a top performer in your organization. In fact, your boss and others have told you that you're a rising star. They said that you can take on more responsibility and that you're on the fast track within your company. You work hard—very hard. What's wrong with putting in some extra hours at night and working some weekends? You reason that, in order to be successful and to move up within the company, it's just part of the deal. But that's OK—you're on the fast track. You're moving up, and you can see a promotion in your near future. You're beaming inside, enjoying the nectar of your success. Life couldn't be any better, right?

Meanwhile, your family sees less and less of you. Plus, you constantly check your cell phone when you get home. Dinners at night with the entire family seldom happen. You're dead tired when you get home, and the last thing you want to do is talk about your day with your spouse. You're doing them a favor, right? All you can think about is scarfing down some food and relaxing in your favorite chair. You can check in with your children tomorrow. You might occasionally miss a ball game or recital, but, hey, you're a successful professional. The kids understand. Your spouse understands—at least that's how you've rationalized your choices. You answer some emails before you turn in for the night. It just goes with the territory of being a rising star, right?

Could this be you?

Rising Star or Falling Star?

Family is the lifeblood of true happiness in this world, not success yielded from work. It's not the accolades bestowed upon you by others. It's the love you provide to your family, and it's servant leadership within the home. It's talking with your spouse and children and listening to the words they say to you. It's spending true quality time with them. It's showing up at your children's events outside the home—and being on time. It's sharing details about your day with your spouse. It's committing to date nights so that you and your spouse can both stay deeply connected. It's putting family first—always. Work can wait, I promise you. Work may provide you a sense of happiness, but without your family, you miss out on true, deep, and meaningful happiness. Without intentionality, you risk never experiencing it. A rising star at work could become a falling star at home if commitment to your family is lacking.

Faith, Family, Friends, Work— in That Order

It didn't take very long to realize that a rising star was on the leadership team when I started at TriStar Summit Medical Center in 2003. Wendy Brandon, the chief operating officer, was ready and prepared to be a hospital CEO. She had worked hard and achieved much success as she moved up within our company. The question that confronted her was whether to consider CEO openings now or later.

Wendy was well-grounded in her faith, made family and friends a priority, and placed work last in the order of importance. It showed in the way she allocated her time and made decisions. She discovered several opportunities but felt that the timing wasn't right and that it might negatively affect those areas of importance to her. She committed to refining her leadership skills even more, and she stayed with our team for about two more years. She helped me transition into my new role as CEO and contributed significantly to our team's success during that time. She was later promoted to CEO at a hospital in Florida. Her values have remained the same throughout the years, and she now leads a very large and successful healthcare system in Orlando, Florida.

Dinner at the Whitehorn House

I cannot write this section without giving thanks and praise to Jennifer and our two daughters, Ashleigh and Emily. They mean everything to me. Although I had my fair share of working some long hours, my goal was to leave the hospital by 6:30 p.m. Even if they were hungry, they were always willing to wait for me so that we could eat dinner together as a family. Jennifer made this a priority, and I'm eternally grateful to her for doing so. That was our special time each day when we connected and talked as a family. Both girls were excellent students and dancers. They studied hard and practiced ballet, tap, and jazz for multiple hours after school each day. Yes, I admit that I was exhausted and tired at times, and the idea of getting to my chair circulated in my brain. However, we made this our family time. All the credit goes to Jennifer for making this happen. Family first—always.

What Are Your Priorities?

Actions speak louder than words. If employees wish to value their families over work, it starts with the leader. They go as you go. If you place faith, family, friends, and work in this order of priorities, I applaud you. If you're trying to get there, please keep working at it. For others who don't prioritize it this way, my wish is for you to consider it. Your life will be more fulfilled, and you will become a better leader.

Now, what about you?

1. Which truly comes first in your life: family or work?
2. What are you doing to show your team that you place family before work?

4

The Joy of Promoting Others

"The growth and development of people
is the highest calling of leadership."
— Harvey Firestone,
founder, Firestone Tire and Rubber Company

Nine years into my professional career, I was the newly named CEO at TriStar Southern Hills Medical Center in Nashville. I had just started two days earlier. My normal routine when starting as the new CEO was to spend thirty minutes with each of the hospital department directors within the first week. My goal? I assessed each leader to determine if they had a positive attitude, a commitment to teamwork, and a burning passion to win. I needed to know where they stood on these key attributes in order to assemble the best team possible. I could only do this by asking them powerful questions and evaluating their answers.

Maybe it wasn't completely fair to draw a conclusion so quickly, but I decided all of this in that thirty-minute meeting. It was probably more like an interview, but it was a vital meeting. Most likely, the department leaders had no idea how critical this meeting was. It determined whether or not they were on the new team I was assembling. Fair or unfair, that's how I did it. I didn't have a lot of time because a new leader's honeymoon period doesn't last long. A strong team was fundamentally important to achieve success.

What Did You Just Say?

The meeting with one director in particular went very well—the leader of food and nutrition services. He managed his department superbly. He spoke highly of his team. He gave them credit for the department's success rather than himself. He knew his operational numbers. He voiced some really good ideas. He was clearly a team player. I liked his competitive spirit. He checked all the boxes. He passed the interview and was on the new team.

At the end of the meeting, he asked me, in a rather nervous tone, if I planned to hire an assistant administrator. Because of the hospital's challenging financial condition, I had already decided that I would not fill that role. He then stunned me by saying that he wanted the job. I was taken aback. *What? Did you not hear me? There is no job.* What's more, the traditional career track for someone wishing to advance to a hospital CEO did not start as a director of food and nutritional services. I knew of no one who had ever advanced from this role to an assistant administrator, much less to a CEO.

"What did you say?" I replied, with my eyes squinted and my face a display of shock. "I just told you that I'm not filling the role right now."

He looked me straight in the eyes, and then he respectfully replied with an answer that absolutely floored me: "I'm going to wear you down."

Wear me down? Are you kidding? Man, that's gutsy. You've only known me for forty-eight hours, and you're telling me that you're going to wear ME down?

Well, he ultimately did! He indeed wore me down. This young man was eager to learn and advance. Any project that I didn't have time to complete, he took. When I needed to delegate a task to someone, he accepted. And guess what? He asked for more. He possessed an insatiable desire to learn. I was impressed—very impressed.

Fast forward: In time, I promoted him to assistant administrator. He did so well that he was subsequently promoted several more times, each time to a larger hospital with more responsibility. Not only did he advance to become a hospital CEO, he became a great hospital CEO. He far exceeded my expectations. Today, Mark Sims serves as CEO for one of HCA's most successful hospitals. I couldn't be prouder of him. I always enjoyed promoting members of the team. I love it when great things happen to great people.

The Joy of Promoting Others

One of the most intrinsic rewards for a leader is to promote a member of their team and to watch them succeed. It's hard to put into words the strong sense of pride that swelled when I saw others on our team promoted. Their hard work changed their lives, their families' lives, and the lives of those they led. The goal was for them to do the same thing for others, to develop them and give them opportunities to advance.

Sure, it can be challenging for bosses in the short term. You're now down a person until you can fill the role. You have to spend extra hours with the new person you hire. Your own productivity declines. But isn't it all worth it? Isn't it great to see others succeed? Never forget how grateful you were when someone gave you a chance. Pass along this gift to others.

Help Those Who Help You

As leaders, we all know we wouldn't be where we are if not for the help of others. Yes, we were promoted, but not by ourselves. Your team members need your help, too. Consider the following:

1. Invest your time and energy to develop leaders who desire to advance in their careers.
2. Do the same for those who want to improve yet stay in their current roles. They deserve your attention and support, too.
3. Never be the selfish leader who holds their people back for your own personal gain.
4. Celebrate the successes of those who advance but move on from your team.
5. Give back to your company by preparing future leaders who will keep the company moving forward after you are no longer there.

Although you may never hear the words "I'm going to wear you down" from one of your young leaders, it's highly likely a few of them are thinking it. People on your team want a shot, a chance to advance. Give it to them. Great leaders love to promote others, even if it means those staff members must leave their current team in order to advance. Staff deserve it. Your company benefits tremendously. Great leaders get this. Celebrate the success of others! Don't miss the opportunity to change lives. Be on the lookout for those who are determined to wear you down. They just may be your best leaders for the future.

Now, what about you?

1. What are you doing to help each member of your team grow and develop professionally?
2. How can you more effectively create more leaders from your team?

#5

Expect Forks in the Road

"On every journey you take, you are met
with options. At every fork in the road,
you make a choice. These are the decisions
that shape your life."
— Mike DeWine, governor of Ohio

It was a day that had been filled with conflicting emotions. I had interviewed for an open CEO position at a small community hospital in rural Kentucky, about an hour away from a large city. The interview had gone extremely well from my perspective. The regional vice president of the company indicated that I was his choice for the job. I was thrilled.

It was 1994, and I was the COO at Doctors Hospital in Columbus, Georgia. I was thirty-two years old, and the opportunity was before me: I was interviewing for my first hospital CEO role at HCA. This was the promotion I needed to advance my career. I had worked hard to get to this point, and now it was here. It was my time to lead. Hard work and sacrifice had paid off. It was a great feeling. I was happy, especially for me.

Quite inwardly focused.

However, there were some drawbacks. The hospital was located about five hundred miles from where we currently lived. We didn't know a soul in the small town, nor anyone in the larger city nearby. No family near us. I rationalized that we had relocated several times in the past, and we could do it again. I was totally focused on myself.

There was one big, very important variable that was different from all the other times we had relocated: Jennifer was four months pregnant with our first child. We had waited ten years before deciding to have children. This was an extremely special time in our lives. Was now truly the right time to move so far away? And with no family or friends nearby? Was this fair to Jennifer?

A real estate agent gave us a tour around the small town and showed us a few houses. Although it was a pretty town, and several nice houses had For Sale signs in their front yards, something still gnawed at me. Jennifer remained encouraging, but I could sense that she was not at peace.

That night, as we ate dinner, we spoke very few words. Though she did her best to hide it, I could tell Jennifer was troubled. She had always encouraged me and been by my side in every move that we had made in order to advance my career. However, this time was different—very different. We were about to start a family. I could see a fork in the road ahead: professional advancement or family priorities.

The final straw that convinced us that this was not the correct move happened at church that night. We visited a mid-sized congregation. Members were talkative, but only with each other in small groups in the foyer. We assembled in the auditorium for the service, then found an adult class afterward on our own. No one offered to give us directions even though we had the look of "where are we going?" on our faces.

The strangest thing occurred that evening: No one said hello or introduced themselves. Not a person! I couldn't believe it. Not so much as a head nod. Nothing. How could we relocate to a city where we knew no one, Jennifer was four months pregnant, and the church we attended was the unfriendliest congregation we've ever visited in our lives?

Confronting the Fork in the Road

I had to confront this major fork in the road and go one way or the other: family or career advancement. Frankly, as the day unfolded, it became an easy decision. Family comes first, and the timing for such a move was horrible. Plus, I don't think that we would have been happy there. Easy call. Although I received the fiercest, loudest, and most intense chewing out from the regional vice president that I ever incurred in my entire career, I was at peace. Call me what you want Mr. Regional Vice President, but I made the right call.

As a leader, you will encounter forks in the road. Count on it. Every professional does, and so will you. Yes, there are other forks in the road, such as choosing which college to attend, whom to marry, where to live, and so on. In your professional career, however, there will only be a few major forks in the road, but they will impact you and your career greatly. Most likely they will deal with your current job, a promotion within the company, or a job opportunity outside the company.

Navigating Forks in the Road

So how does one go about deciding which road to take? You are the person who knows your situation the best. Consider asking yourself the following questions in order to help you make your decision:

1. **What are the pros and cons of the job?** Go old-school and take a sheet of paper, draw a line down the middle, then write the pros on the left side and cons on the right side. Weight them, if needed. How does it add up? What's it telling you?

2. **How will my family be affected by the new job?** In other words, think outwardly, not inwardly. Talk with your spouse. Talk with your children. If relocation is involved, how will this affect them? I once knew a CEO who moved his family when his daughter was a rising senior in high school. They relocated to a city where she knew no one. She had to leave all her friends during a critical time in her life. When he shared this story, his daughter had not spoken a word to him in five years. How tragic. There is not a job in this world worth that consequence.

3. **What is the culture like at the prospective company?** Do your homework. Ask around. Ask current employees of the new company. Sense it when you interview.

4. **How will I grow as a leader if I accept the new job?** There's no reason to take a promotion or change jobs if neither one provides you with current and future growth opportunities.

5. **Have I prayed for guidance?** Praying to God for guidance and wisdom will help you in your decision-making. He knows the future—you don't.

Are You Ready?

Your professional journey will have some ups and downs, some twists and turns, and some forks in the road. They are stressful times where effective decision-making is absolutely critical. Ask yourself the questions above, and let your answers guide you toward the best decision.

Now, what about you?

1. What's the one question you can ask yourself that will best help you face a fork in the road?
2. What do you consider to be most important in helping you decide which direction to go when there is a fork in the road?

#6

Develop Executive Presence

"Executive presence is credibility
that goes beyond a title."
— Tom Henschel, president and
leadership coach, Essential Communications

A number of years ago, I interviewed a man for a leadership position on our team at TriStar Summit Medical Center. He had an impressive resume that showed a number of accomplishments in his career. He came highly recommended by a trusted friend and colleague who had good judgment about people and talent. It's no surprise that I was excited about his interest in the job.

After he arrived, I came out of my office to greet him. "Hello, I'm Jeff Whitehorn," I said. He replied in a somewhat condescending tone, "I see that you are." *I see that you are? What kind of response is that when you meet someone for the first time?* His response felt rather pompous. Strike one.

I invited him into my office and asked him to sit down at the round table. He then proceeded to take off his coat and hang it on the back of his chair. He slumped down in the chair and crossed one leg over the other. Wow, his self-confidence was overflowing! *Who is that comfortable in a first interview?* He didn't smile but had an arrogant look. I couldn't believe what I was seeing. *Who is interviewing whom?* Another display of cockiness. Strike two.

I then opened with a softball question: "Please tell me a little about yourself." He proceeded to go on and on about his education and all his professional successes. I thought he would never stop. I kept thinking, *When is this guy going to pause to take a breath?* Not one time during his long-winded monologue did he ever acknowledge his team—he took all the credit. His favorite words seemed to be "I" and "my." He bragged about himself constantly. Strike three. Interview over.

I was done. Zero self-awareness on his part. No place for him on our team.

This man lacked *executive presence.*

The Importance of Executive Presence

Executive presence is a set of leadership skills that formulate the way others view and judge you as a leader. It contributes to your personal brand. Some people call them "soft skills." I call them "must-have" skills. You need them to win.

Improving executive presence is one of the most frequently requested coaching goals that I encounter with my clients. It's a somewhat overlooked skill set that is vital to one's ability to be hired or promoted.

How important is executive presence to your career? Research performed by Coqual (formerly Center for Talent Innovation) concluded that executive presence accounts for as much as 28 percent of what it takes to get promoted into leadership positions.[1] Wow! Think about that for a moment. You may be the smartest leader there is, but a lack of executive presence can possibly hold you back from advancing in your career.

The Role of Self-Confidence

Perhaps the most powerful component of executive presence is self-confidence. You have to have it. The key, however, is to not go overboard. There's a difference between displaying genuine self-confidence and being cocky. No one likes a leader who is cocky. Arrogance does not inspire others—it actually works against a leader. I believe that arrogance is often a sign of insecurity.

On the other hand, swagger is a notch or two below cocky. Swagger isn't bad if held in check. The problem lies in the fact that it's really close to arrogance. It's all about how that swagger is perceived by others. Be careful with swagger.

Genuine confidence comes from the heart. It's a natural instinct of being true to oneself. It's believing in your God-given abilities. It comes through experience—a number of successes along the way builds your confidence. Genuine confidence is respected by your supervisor, colleagues, and direct reports. It is the cornerstone of executive presence.

Other key areas of executive presence include asking questions at meetings, operating well under stress, dressing for success, communicating effectively, and listening actively.

---

1 "Do You Have Executive Presence?" *Marie Claire*, November 2012, https://www.marieclaire.com/career-advice/tips/a7342/do-you-have-executive-presence.

Ask Questions at Meetings

One of the quickest and easiest ways to improve your executive presence is asking at least one question at every meeting you attend. It can be your meeting, your boss's meeting, your colleague's meeting, your company's meeting, and so on. Asking a question at every meeting is important because you're showing proper respect to the speaker. You're truly listening. The reward is that everyone else in the room concludes those same things about you. Your executive presence is reinforced.

Another meeting tip is to occasionally use a powerful nonverbal communication technique that I call "Spider on the Mirror." I learned this from a college professor at the University of Alabama while working on my MBA, and it is gold! While sitting at the conference table, place your fingers and thumbs from both hands together, and slowly press in and out. Visualize a spider on a mirror. This is a powerful nonverbal tool that communicates to others that you are keenly listening to every word and truly pondering what they are saying. It displays confidence and understanding, a powerful form of executive presence.

Stay Calm under Pressure

Operating well under stress affects your executive presence. Everyone is watching you. Do you remain calm or fly off the handle? Do you listen to others or hunker down alone? Do you blame others or take ownership of the situation? Do you make timely decisions and take action, or do you delay taking action by seeking more and more information? Consider asking for feedback from others to determine how you are perceived as a leader during stressful situations.

Dress for Success

Although times have changed regarding proper business attire, make no mistake—others judge you by what you wear. Fair or unfair, it affects what others think of you and impacts your executive presence. The best advice that I can pass along comes from the book *How to Become a Rainmaker* by Jeffrey J. Fox. His advice is to always dress a little bit better than your customer. This can also apply to those you lead. Neither underdress nor overdress. Just slightly better. It shows your customer respect while positively impacting your executive presence.

Communicate Effectively and Listen Actively

Effective communication and active listening are major drivers of executive presence, so much so that each deserves its own separate chapter. Stay tuned.

I cannot emphasize enough the importance of developing your executive presence. Make it one of your top development goals. Great leaders have executive presence. Good leaders want it. Bad leaders have no clue.

Now, what about you?

1. What area of executive presence do you feel most needs improvement?
2. How do others view you when you are under stress? How do you know?

#7

Be Strong and Courageous

"Have I not commanded you?
Be strong and courageous. Do not be afraid;
do not be discouraged, for the LORD your God
will be with you wherever you go."
— Joshua 1:9 (NIV)

I knew I had my work cut out for me. Although I had been a hospital CEO for several years, I had not encountered what I was now facing. I was the new CEO of a hospital that had been struggling for a couple of years, especially the previous few months before I arrived. Its profitability had declined approximately 33 percent in just one year. It was no surprise that patient satisfaction ranked near the bottom. It was a mess. I had just relocated my family six months previously. *What have I gotten myself into?*

When I started, I met a number of really good hospital employees and physicians. Unfortunately, that wasn't the case across the board. I encountered some employees and doctors who were quite vocal and negative. Apathy among some staff was evident. It was extremely clear that the hospital's culture, vision, communication, and strategic plan had to change. However, we had a nucleus of talented leaders who could be the foundation on which to build a really good team. In spite of the obstacles, I was very optimistic.

Two hospital service lines needed major improvement. Patient volumes had been low for quite some time. Many physicians who practiced solely at the hospital referred their patients who needed these specialized services to doctors at other hospitals. When I sought feedback from our hospital leaders about these service lines, they admitted that they, too, referred their own family and friends to other doctors who didn't practice at the hospital. This was quite troubling.

I discussed the situation with the doctors of the two under-performing service lines. Their reaction caught me a little off guard. They blamed everything on the hospital. They blamed administration, which is basically the CEO. They blamed hospital employees. They blamed the location of the hospital. They blamed hospital marketing. They took absolutely zero ownership of the problem. They truly believed it was everyone else's fault.

Time to Take Action

Our team worked hard to revamp the two service lines. We purchased new equipment and improved patient flow. We provided additional training to the hospital staff in these departments. Still, no change in patient volumes. The four specialty physicians adamantly blamed the hospital. They held firm that it was others, not themselves, who had to change. After six months of trying to collaborate with these physicians, I knew it was time to go a different direction, one that was more drastic. Enough was enough—I was done with these four doctors.

The time had come to make the hard call. I decided that the best strategy would be to recruit some new physicians to grow these service lines. Fresh faces and new leadership were the answer. Our community deserved better. Our loyal doctors asked for this change. Solving the problem and taking action was squarely my responsibility. The possible ramifications of this decision, however, made this change in direction extremely risky. My job security could be on the line. I had seen medical staff members turn on a few of my fellow CEOs when the staff felt that a physician was being attacked by the administration. They might not even like that doctor themselves, but they would defend the doctor to no end. Many great hospital CEOs have had to move on because of poor relations with the medical staff. You could be destined to be in the Hospital CEO Hall of Fame, but poor medical staff relations could cost you your job. Nothing personal, but that's just the way it was. That's what I had signed up for when I chose hospital administration as my career. I loved my job, but it certainly carried a level of risk.

Meeting with My Boss

I scheduled a meeting with my boss, Paul Rutledge, our division president, to communicate my recommendation to solve the problem. I knew what we needed to do. It was the right strategy, but it contained a ton of risk. I was quite nervous. *What if the medical staff turned against me?* I had relocated my family just six months prior. I didn't want to move them again if this strategy failed.

When I presented my strategy, Paul sensed that I was nervous. He had been a hospital CEO and knew the pressure of the role. His response was amazing. He said, "I have your back. Don't worry. Do the right thing. Read Joshua 1 in the

Bible when you go home tonight. And remember, I have your back."

That night, I read the whole book of Joshua. Joshua was taking over for Moses to lead the Israelites into the Promised Land. Moses was one of the greatest leaders in the history of the world. Joshua must have been nervous, too. Who wouldn't be? In the first chapter, God tells Joshua, "Be strong and courageous" four times. What a blessing it was to have that support from my boss. That was all I needed. I was pumped and ready to execute the plan.

I communicated to the doctors of these underachieving service lines that I planned to recruit new physicians in their specialty—full disclosure. No more listening to their blame game. It was time to take them head on. They saw this as a hostile move and that it would create competition against them. They were absolutely right! That was my plan.

Over the next few months, these doctors did everything they could to sabotage my plan. I was called about every name in the book, and a couple of them even threatened me. My reaction? *Take a number—my boss has my back!*

The Outcome

Although there were some bumps and bruises along the way, the outcome could not have been better. I recruited two of the best doctors I've ever recruited. Both were highly success-ful. They knew what they were up against, and they gladly accepted the challenge. They wanted to help their patients and to work with the hospital to improve the service lines. Patient volumes soared and increased at a faster rate than anticipated. Those physicians did so well that we had to recruit additional doctors to join their practices.

The Supportive Boss

Every leader has to make tough decisions. Some are more complex and riskier than others. Some are popular while others are not. Working for a boss who has your back is invaluable. It's a priceless gift from a great leader. When times are tough for your leaders, I challenge you to let them know you support them. They deserve to hear you say, "Be strong and courageous." Wouldn't you want to hear the same words from your boss? I did, and it was awesome.

Now, what about you?

1. What actions could you take to let your staff know that you truly support them?
2. How do you create a culture of trust and support among your team?

#8

Never Get Too Down (or Up) on Yourself

"Successful people have fear, successful people
have doubt, and successful people have worry.
They just don't let these feelings stop them."
— T. Harv Eker, author, businessman,
and motivational speaker

It had been an extremely challenging start to the year
in 2016 at TriStar Summit Medical Center. A group of
physicians who ran our inpatient hospitalist program had
recently given notice to terminate their contract. These were
the attending physicians for almost all the medical patients
in the hospital. The impact of this move was like an atomic
bomb had been dropped in the middle of the hospital. It negatively affected almost every department due to confusion
and poor communication. It affected patients, employees,
and physicians. We had to contract with temporary hospitalist physicians until we could recruit new full-time

doctors. This only added to people's frustrations. Employee morale took a nosedive. Finger-pointing abounded. Everyone was frustrated, and I didn't blame them. It was tough, real tough.

A defining moment occurred in a very unexpected way. On top of the inpatient hospitalist program fiasco that loomed over the hospital and consumed my time, I was having one of those days. You know what I mean. We've all had them. Everything, and I mean everything, was going wrong. Bad news hit me when I first walked into the office that Monday morning, and more bad news kept coming my way. I had just lost a physician I was recruiting to a competitor. Several of our specialty physicians were upset about a particular issue, and they didn't hold back when we met that morning.

Later, as I was walking down the hallway, a physician approached me with more bad news. He informed me that his group of physicians had decided to give notice, leave the medical staff, and no longer see patients at our hospital. *What? You've got to be kidding me!* It was devastating. A major strategy to help lead our team out of this mess was dependent on that group of doctors practicing at our hospital. *How could I possibly make this work without them?* I felt so defeated. I texted the group's leader and asked if I could meet him at his office that evening. He agreed.

I drove to his office, which was located on a different hospital campus. My confidence was shaken by the day's events. I walked through the dark parking lot to his office with my tail tucked between my legs. I was literally going to have to beg for the physician group to please stay and practice at our hospital. It was very humbling. I felt beaten and whipped. Fortunately, I had a good working relationship with the leader of the physician group, and I had a plan. After much discussion, he accepted my compromise and the physician group would stay and continue to practice at our hospital. I breathed a huge sigh of relief.

Out of Nowhere

After the meeting, I walked slowly back to my car. I was so tired. I could hardly see in the dark. I was sweating profusely from both the meeting and the stifling humidity. I was feeling as low as I had ever felt in recent memory. I was mentally and physically exhausted. *Just let me get home and see Jennifer*, I thought. Suddenly, I heard a voice somewhere in the parking lot say, "Jeff? Are you Jeff Whitehorn?" Of course, my first reaction was to respond, "Well, it depends." I turned and saw a man in the distance standing by his car with his trunk open. I couldn't see his face very well in the dark. *Who is this?*

I walked toward him. "Yes, that's me. Can I help you?" I responded, somewhat skeptically.

The man said in a very kind and respectful tone, "You might not remember me, but I worked with you while you were the CEO at Southern Hills Medical Center a number of years ago. I just wanted to let you know that it was the best hospital I've ever worked at. I loved the culture, and I loved my team. I've always wanted to thank you for the great job you did."

Wow, what a shot in the arm! That was exactly what I needed to hear. I thanked the man and shook his hand firmly. I could feel the energy returning to my weary body. This man was a godsend. He had no idea what he had done to help me. My outlook changed. Positivity and confidence returned. I walked back to my car with a bit more spring in my step, head up, and shoulders back. I can do this. Thank you, Lord!

Over the next twelve months, the physicians we recruited to form our new hospitalist group exceeded expectations, worked as a team, and delivered great care to the patients. Both employee and physician morale improved remarkably. However, we could never have achieved these results if the other physician group had left. Looking back, I rank that meeting with the group's leader as one of the most crucial ones in my career. No doubt God was with me that night.

A Quote to Remember

Coach Lou Holtz certainly knew the euphoria of winning and the gut-wrenching emotion of losing. Although he was fired from the University of Arkansas in 1983, he went on to win the college football national championship at Notre Dame University in 1988. Was he a good coach or a bad coach? I guess that depends on your perspective, and perhaps on who you root for in college football. Nonetheless, his overall coaching record as a college coach was 249-132-7—not too shabby. Plus, he wears a college football national championship ring.

One of my all-time favorite quotes by Coach Holtz is this: "You're never as good as they say you are when you win, and you're never as bad as they say you are when you lose." As a leader, when you're producing great operational results, improving employee engagement and teamwork, and increasing market share, you are a genius. Just ask others as they pile on the praise. On the other hand, when you're not delivering good financial results, employee morale is slipping, or market share is declining, you are an idiot. Ironically, this conclusion is made by some of the same people who called you a genius the previous year!

Consistency Is Elusive

That's just the way it works these days, unfortunately. Everyone wants to win, and they want to win now. You're the boss. You're accountable. But consistently winning year after year is hard. In fact, it's very hard.

I once thought that going into an underperforming hospital and turning it around was the most challenging job of all. I loved coming in, developing the team, formulating and implementing a new strategy, and achieving strong results. It was hard work but very rewarding. Nothing could be harder than this, at least in my mind. My thinking changed when I stayed at the next hospital for a longer period of time. Consistently producing outstanding results year after year was far more difficult. Staying on top is so challenging! That's why there are very few dynasties.

Average leaders read and believe their own press clippings. They believe all the great things said about them when things are working well. Then their heads swell. There's trouble ahead. There will be an occasional down year. It's ego-piercing to the average leader to then be looked upon as underperforming. *What? I'm not as great as they said I was last year? It just can't be!* And then there's the sound of their ego crashing.

Everything cycles. Great leaders understand this. Stay grounded. Never get too down or too up on yourself. Remember the quote from Coach Holtz. He knew what he was talking about.

Now, what about you?

1.   How do you overcome times of self-doubt?
2.   How do you help others overcome their self-doubt?

9

Saturate Them with Effective Communication

"Seek first to understand, then to be understood."
— Stephen Covey, author,
The 7 Habits of Highly Effective People

The meeting was finally here. It had taken me almost two months to coordinate everyone's calendar. The audience: the market president, the division president, and the group president. All the bosses present at the same time at the hospital. My mission: Obtain the group president's approval to fund a strategically important project at our growing hospital in Nashville. The stakes were high. This might be my only shot. *Make it count, Whitehorn.*

There was one small problem, possibly a big problem if I didn't communicate the message correctly. In my preparation for the presentation, I sought input and feedback from both the market and division presidents. In doing so, I realized that we were not all three quite in alignment as to the flow of the presentation nor the main points to be emphasized.

The question: How do I articulate the presentation to the group president in a way that pleases everyone? I was confident that I could do it. That was my first mistake.

Showtime

Within the first five minutes of the meeting, I could sense that it wasn't going well. In fact, it was going south quickly. The group president peppered me with questions—all very fair questions. I stumbled, focusing more on the problems rather than the solutions. I deviated from the script, thinking my answers would please the market and division presidents. Instead, they were vague and unclear. Bad move on my part. That was my second mistake.

Then came the moment of truth. The group president paused. Silence filled the room. His steely eyes stared straight at me. I knew right away that whatever he was about to say was not going to be good.

He then uttered these stinging five words: "I'm saturated with the problems." Ouch! I had never heard that phrase before, and it was directed squarely at me. That phrase was forever seared into my brain. *What should I say?* Pure silence followed as I waited for his next sentence. My only response was to acknowledge he was correct and retreat, and quickly.

Needless to say, he didn't approve the project that evening. I communicated the message poorly. I rambled more about the problems rather than the solutions. I did an inadequate job of anticipating questions. The list goes on.

Effective Communication

Outstanding communication is more than just making presentations. It's listening to others, asking questions, and clearly articulating your message. It's keeping bosses above you, peers beside you, and team members below you informed on current issues and future goals. It's understanding and interpreting the nonverbal communication from others, such as body language.

Effective communication is critical to the success of a great leader, and I mean critical. It provides clear direction to your team. It motivates them. It inspires them. It increases job satisfaction and performance. Poor communication, on the other hand, will frustrate your team. They hate it. They grumble behind your back. Ultimately, they will quit on you and leave. Wouldn't you?

Communication is also a major driver of a great culture. Staff want to hear you articulate your vision. Your team wants to know where the organization is headed. They want to know how they contribute to your vision. Clearly communicate this to them over and over.

What Can I Do?

Strong communicators do the following:

1. **Practice MBWA (Management by Wandering Around).** Tom Peters wrote about this in his groundbreaking book, *In Search of Excellence.* Just wandering around while listening and talking to staff is a very powerful form of communication. Plus, your team loves it.

2. **Stay connected virtually.** COVID-19 has impacted

the workplace like nothing else. Specifically, it has forced leaders to adjust their communication methods. Communicating virtually is the norm for a rising number of people. More people now work from home, and this trend will continue. Embrace it.

3. **Seek input from their team by asking questions.** They value their team's insights and perspectives. Asking questions eliminates confusion and provides clarity.

4. **Deliver powerful presentations to both large and small groups.** They utilize good eye contact, speak slowly, and know how to read their audience. They understand that audiences prefer storytelling over boring slides showing hundreds of itty-bitty numbers they can hardly read. They use humor appropriately but understand that it can be risky.

5. **Acknowledge the need to use multiple communication methods.** Different generations sometimes prefer different forms of communication. For example, baby boomers normally prefer face-to-face communication while Gen Xers like phone, email, and text communication.

6. **Love to slay rumors within the organization.** Embrace that rumors exist. Take them head on and address them.

7. **Use brevity in their emails and texts.** They understand that this form of communication can easily be misinterpreted at times. Consider going old-school and make a phone call. It saves valuable time and provides clarity.

Learn from Others

The absolute master of presentations is Louis Joseph, group vice president, Physician Services Group, at HCA. I've known Louis for more than thirty years. He has the gift of delivering a message in such a way that the audience stays engaged throughout his entire presentation. He uses humor and storytelling. He incorporates slides that show pictures or quotes rather than boring lines of small rows of numbers. I've learned how to deliver better presentations just by watching him. My challenge to you is to do the same—learn from someone you believe is a great communicator.

One Last Bit of Saturation

Following my unsuccessful presentation to our group president, he called me the next day. He gave me valuable feedback on how to improve my presentation skills. Good news was that he was laughing while he spoke, especially after I complimented him on his use of the word "saturated." I was blessed that he took the time to give me constructive feedback. That was a class act by a great leader. Within sixty days, he approved the project. It was a valuable lesson learned with a positive outcome. It doesn't always happen that way. I got lucky.

Want to become a better leader? Then become a better communicator.

Now, what about you?

1. What could you do today in order to become a better communicator?
2. When was the last time you asked for feedback from others on your communication skills?

10

You're the New Leader —Now What?

"Stand up to your obstacles and do something
about them. You will find that they haven't
half the strength you think they have."
— Norman Vincent Peale,
minister and author

My meeting with three primary care physicians was booked for 6:00 p.m. that evening in their office. These doctors weren't just ordinary members of the medical staff; they were THE informal group leaders of the medical staff. If you wanted something done, you had to have their support. They strongly influenced most of the other doctors. Of course, jealousy and pride caused several of the other doctors to dislike them—behind their backs, of course. Nevertheless, the group was powerful. This was a critical meeting. It needed to go well. Significant changes had to be made at the hospital, and I needed their help. To say that this was a crucial conversation would be a huge understatement. Personally, I was a little nervous. Who wouldn't be, right?

I had been appointed CEO in 1996 at this small, sixty-bed hospital in rural Georgia about one month prior to this meeting. It was my first time to lead as CEO at a medical/surgical hospital. When I arrived, the hospital had a grand total of eight patients. Not surprisingly, it was extremely under budget from a financial perspective. I had my work cut out for me. There was only one way to go, and that was up, or at least that's what I thought.

The CEO position at this hospital was not one of the most desired jobs within the company. In addition to the low number of patients, the hospital was dysfunctional in so many ways. Frankly, it was a train wreck. However, I had been given the opportunity to serve as the hospital CEO, and I jumped on it. *I can do this. I can bridge the vast chasm between the hospital and the physicians. I know that I can put a strong team together and implement a new strategic direction.* However, I needed these three doctors on my side to help make it happen. If not, making changes would be difficult.

The Meeting Begins

We exchanged pleasantries at the beginning. Small talk consisted of learning more about one another, families, and hobbies. I knew that many CEOs had come and gone since they began practicing together twenty years ago. The hospital had been sold several times. I sensed a severe lack of trust. Even though I knew I would shoot straight with them, they didn't know that. They had been burned in the past. How could I build trust, and quickly?

We-Be's

It was time to get down to business. One of the doctors, probably the most gregarious of the three, leaned across the table and stared at me. He was silent—just kept staring at me, straight in the eyes. No sound, slight smile. It felt like time had stood still. He then uttered these resounding words in a strong tone: "Son, we are 'we-be's'. Do you know what we-be's are?"

"No, sir, I don't," I replied.

"Let me tell you then. *We be* here before you got here. *We be* here while you're here. And *we be* here when you're gone. Got that?"

Loud and clear, I thought. It was at that moment that I knew my stay as CEO at this hospital was not going to be long term. Nope, my job would be to clean up the mess and get the hospital back on track for future success. My job was to make the hospital better than it was when I took over. No need to put together a five-year strategic plan. Nope, just get in there, get my hands dirty, and fix the problems, then get ready for the next assignment from HCA. That meeting was a learning experience.

The story ended pretty well, however. Although the three physicians didn't do much to help fix the problems, they didn't stand in the way of what had to be done. Our team worked hard to help start a change in the culture of the hospital and the relationship with the medical staff. Over time, more patients chose not to leave the community for their healthcare. Rather, they chose our hospital. Subsequently, patient volume grew to a level not seen in years. A number of physicians got on board with what we were doing and supported us. A few others watched and grumbled on the sidelines. When I left a year later, the patient census was up to twenty-two patients per day. I credit the team for the volume turnaround. It wasn't easy, but the hospital was a better place than when I started. Mission accomplished.

What Did I Learn?

When you're a new leader, not everyone is going to trust you nor follow you right from the outset. Developing trust takes time, but you can still set and achieve high operational goals. At times, half the fun is simply "finding a way to win." That phrase is overused in sports all the time but it's true—great teams just have a knack for winning. As the leader, you keep trying things to see what will work as you build trust with your team over time. Moving everyone toward a common goal starts with trust. Trust starts with building strong relationships.

Being the new leader of a team is fun on one hand, but extremely challenging on the other. It's exhilarating to be the person to lead the way, but it comes with a lot of responsibility. In the beginning, some new leaders struggle and wonder what they should do first and how to do it. For someone who is a brand-new leader, it can be very intimidating.

What Can You Do?

Here are some effective actions that you can take as the new leader in order to get off to a strong start with your new team:

1. Build trust with all stakeholders.
2. Find a quick and easy win.
3. Articulate your vision, but not until after you've asked for the team's input.
4. Ask questions—lots of questions.
5. Overcommunicate.
6. Be decisive.

7. Accept that you don't have all the answers, and that's OK.

8. Acknowledge that not everyone is going to gladly help you get the organization where you want it to go.

You are now in charge, and it's your responsibility to move your department or organization forward. Starting strong is imperative. In fact, it's a must. Your team wants to be heard, so listen. They want to see you take action. Do something, and do it quickly. Build trust. Find the quick win. As for the we-be's of the world, just smile and say thank you, then move on and do what you need to do to successfully lead your team. They enjoy complaining almost as much as they enjoy doing nothing. Identify those who will help you achieve your goals and lead away. Don't look back. Trust me on this one.

Now, what about you?

1. What can you do to overcome the "we-be's" of the world?

2. How do you develop trust with all stakeholders?

#11

Delegate More
to Achieve More

"If you want to do a few small things right,
do them yourself. If you want to do great things
and make a big impact, learn to delegate."
— John C. Maxwell, author,
Developing the Leaders Around You

I was twenty-six years old, sitting in the ballroom at the local Holiday Inn in Macon, Georgia. Nothing fancy but I thought this was big-time back then. It was about 7:30 a.m. I had just eaten my second free Krispy Kreme doughnut that morning (oh, how I miss those high metabolism days of yore) when my new boss sat down and joined me. The name of the workshop: "The Art of Delegation."

This was my first job out of graduate school in 1988, and this was my first workshop as the new assistant administrator at Charter Lake Hospital. I was quite jazzed with my new job. *I'm now in the healthcare industry!* This was also the first time I had responsibility for managing others. Frankly, I had no clue. Sad thing is that I had no clue that I had no clue.

I knew absolutely nothing about leading others in a work environment. Sure, I had managed one person on a few auditing engagements as a CPA, and I had led others in different initiatives in college and high school. I had taken college and graduate school classes on leadership and organizational development. This was different, however. I was now in the "real world." Personally, I was a little nervous. People were reporting to me. *Am I really ready for this?*

My new boss told me that one of the keys to being a great leader was being a great delegator. They went hand in hand. I had no idea how profound that statement was. He admitted that this was an area in which he could improve, and he felt that I could learn from this workshop, too. I appreciated his honesty and vulnerability.

Little did I know that this inexpensive $79 seminar would be one of the most powerful workshops, if not the best, that I ever attended in my career. It greatly impacted me. I learned that a productive leader had to delegate more to achieve more.

Four Tools to Improve Delegation

Here are the four tools that I learned about delegation and put into practice:

1. The Urgent/Important Matrix
2. The "What can I live with?" question
3. The 80/20 rule for delegation
4. The best response to block upward delegation

The **Urgent/Important Matrix** is an outstanding tool that can help you identify which tasks can be delegated to others. President Dwight Eisenhower originally developed the concept while serving as a five-star general during World War II, which is now known as the Eisenhower Matrix. Stephen Covey popularized the concept in his 1989 landmark book, *The 7 Habits of Highly Effective People*. He called it the Time Management Matrix.

Today, it's also referred to as the Urgent/Important Matrix. Job tasks are placed into one of four quadrants based on importance and urgency. Tasks assigned to the Delegate quadrant should be delegated to others. If done correctly, this matrix strongly increases your delegation effectiveness.

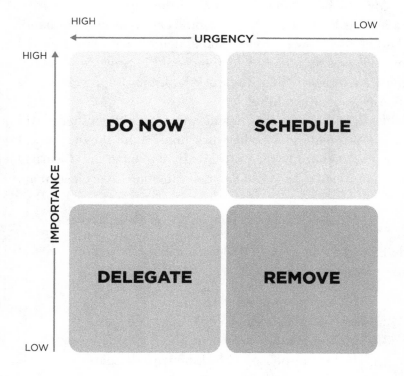

The **"What can I live with?" question** is what you ask yourself when you see the results from the person to whom you delegated the task. If numbers and percentages are involved, they have to be 100 percent correct. But can you live with the minor differences in how it's completed, compared to how you would have done it? It might not be exactly your method or process, but it works. Can you live with this? If you can, and you don't "get the shakes" when work is returned to you, this strategy will save you time.

The **80/20 rule for delegation** says that employees will begin to push back at 80 percent of their work capacity. Therefore, keep delegating a little more to them. They still have the capacity to take on another task or project.

Finally, there's a fantastic strategy to use whenever a direct report drops a problem in your lap, expecting you to fix it. In other words, they delegate upward. Many managers add it to their list of things to do and waste valuable time solving the issue. They believe they can fix it faster or they are the only person who can solve the problem. **The best response to block upward delegation** is to give the problem back to them. Don't own it. Ask them to provide you three options on how to solve the problem and then to recommend which one to implement. Watch their face when you do this the first time! Think about the beauty of this strategy: You help your direct report develop their critical thinking skills while you avoid expending needless energy on tasks that can be completed by others. A bonus: The employee takes ownership of the recommendation they made, and now they take pride in implementing the solution. It's a win-win for everyone.

Great Delegation Is Key to Success

Want to move up in your organization? Learn to delegate. Want to develop your team? Learn to delegate. Want more time to focus on what you are paid to do as a leader? Learn to delegate. Finally, do you strive to be a great leader? Then delegate more to achieve more.

Now, what about you?

1. How do you rank yourself on your ability to delegate?
2. Which tool noted above can you implement to improve your delegation effectiveness?

#12

Always Hire a Winner

*"You were born a winner, but to be a winner,
you must plan to win, prepare to win,
and expect to win."*
— Zig Ziglar, author, salesperson,
and motivational speaker

One year for Christmas, Jennifer gave me a framed print containing a famous motivational quote made by Paul "Bear" Bryant, the highly successful former head football coach at the University of Alabama. It read: "If you believe in yourself and have dedication and pride—and never quit— you'll be a winner. The price of victory is high but so are the rewards."

This print hung in my office for more than twenty years. Every so often, I would look up from my desk and read the quote. It always gave me inspiration. My wife knows me better than anyone else, and she knew that quote would motivate me when I needed a little jolt of encouragement from time to time.

The print was strategically placed in my office so that

others could see it and, hopefully, read it. I felt like it stated what I wanted to be. It reinforced the idea that dedication to excellence in both life and work was needed to achieve success. I was taught that you had to work hard to be successful. No promises, but if you worked hard, you positioned yourself to win. I knew what it felt like to win, and I knew what it felt like to lose. I sure liked winning way more than losing. But then, who doesn't?

That quote packed a lot of punch. At times, those words uplifted me when I needed it. It reminded me of what it took to be a winner. Being crowned champion doesn't come without a price. Hard work and sacrifice are involved.

Assembling Your Team

I soon learned as a leader that, in order to be a winner, I had to surround myself with other winners. I had heard this truth from professors in graduate school numerous times. I had read it in books and articles. However, I didn't understand how true this advice was until I was in charge of leading people and hiring others to be part of our team.

I would love to say that I was 100 percent accurate on all the people I hired over the years. Unfortunately, that wasn't the case. Although I got far more right than wrong, I missed the mark on a few people. It always gnawed at me whenever that happened. In fact, it really ticked me off. I was responsible for the mistake. I felt that I had let the team down whenever that happened, so I committed to learning from each mistake.

Past Experience Required

While at TriStar Southern Hills Medical Center in 2000, a position came open within the marketing department that I deemed critical toward helping execute our strategic plan. Hiring the right person to be assistant marketing director was important. Therefore, I felt strongly that any candidate applying for the position needed past work experience in marketing.

The marketing director was outstanding at her job. She had contributed significantly to growing the business at the hospital. She had very good judgment, and I trusted her. She knew right away who she wanted to hire—there was no reason to interview the long list of applicants. In her mind, she knew she had the right person for the job. The only hurdle she had to overcome was to convince me of her selection. You see, the candidate she knew would be successful had no experience in hospital marketing. In fact, she had only graduated from college a year earlier. I couldn't help but question the marketing director on why she would want to hire someone with no experience.

After a lot of griping, I agreed to interview the candidate even though I knew there was no way we were going to hire her. I was convinced she didn't have a clue about how to market a hospital. How could someone right out of college, with zero experience, be successful in this role? The marketing director assured me that the candidate was the perfect person. As far as I was concerned, this was going to be a courtesy interview, one of which I'm not a fan.

Open Mouth, Insert Foot

Well, I was wrong—completely wrong. Jessica Florida, the inexperienced candidate that I didn't want to interview, did an excellent job that day. She was polished, poised, and professional. Her answers to my questions were spot on. I liked her competitive spirit. I liked her ideas. Indeed, she was the perfect person for the job. We hired her, and to no one's surprise, she was very successful. So much so that she was promoted just a couple of years later to director of marketing at a new sister hospital in our market. She continued to advance within HCA, and today she is a highly successful vice president in physician recruiting.

What Did I Learn?

It was quite humbling to realize I was wrong to insist that every candidate must have past work experience to be considered. Sure, I'm a big believer in hiring teammates who have experience, as it usually increases the odds for success. However, sometimes you should hire a person who has the talent to be a great leader in the future.

Here are my takeaways:

1. People with no experience are often hungrier for success than others.
2. People with a positive attitude and who want to learn can contribute to team goals quickly.
3. Take a chance and hire for future talent.
4. Always hire a winner.

She's a Winner

Fast forward seventeen years to my retirement party in 2017. During a time of storytelling and reflection, Jessica raised her hand to speak. Little did I know that she was about to tell a story that she had not revealed until that night.

About a year after she had been hired, she found an old file folder in the marketing office while she was culling files to throw away. Before tossing it, she noticed her name on the file tab. When she opened the file, it contained the resume from her interview with a yellow Post-it Note attached, one that happened to have my name printed at the top. I had returned this file to the marketing director with a note that read: "Hire her. She's a winner."

I believe Coach Bryant knew a thing or two about what it takes to be a winner. If you're going to be a successful leader, always hire a winner.

Now, what about you?

1. Have you ever settled for an average leader quickly rather than waiting to hire a winner? How did that work out?
2. What can you do to always hire a winner?

#13

Build a Culture
They Will Remember

"Culture outperforms strategy every time.
Culture with strategy is unbeatable."
— Quint Studer, founder, Studer Group

Shortly before I retired, I ran into a former employee and her mother in the lobby of TriStar Summit Medical Center. It had been more than fifteen years since we had worked together at TriStar Southern Hills Medical Center, also in Nashville. She updated me on her family and where she was in her career. She kindly introduced me to her precious mother. She told her mother that there were three things about working at Southern Hills that she would remember forever: It had the "best culture ever," that I knew all the employees by their first names, and that I was the only person she had ever known who didn't own a pair of blue jeans! *Say what?!*

Amazing what people remember, and how rumors get started. I was honored about what she said about the culture and knowing employees' first names. My heart beamed. However, she wasn't quite right about me not owning a single pair of blue jeans—that was just a rumor. I owned several pairs of blue jeans, thank you very much! This rumor most likely started because I was not a big fan of the occasional Blue Jeans Day at the hospital. I was still pretty old-school back then. Our team loved this day, but I was never completely comfortable with it, and usually just wore a pair of khakis. Oh, well.

As I walked away, I thought about what she said about our culture. I reflected on some of the great things we had achieved as a team: we increased our market share, grew our patient volumes, recruited many new physicians, and added new service lines. But what did she remember most? Our culture. She never forgot our teamwork, celebrations, family atmosphere, and genuine respect for each other. It wasn't the tangible results that I thought defined success. Rather, it was the positive intangibles of the organization, starting with culture. That's what she loved, and that's what she remembered.

Positive Influences on Culture

Have you thought about what influences the culture where you work? There are a number of things that can positively impact culture. I believe it's vital to excel in the following four:

1. Living the values of the organization
2. Creating a family-first atmosphere
3. Celebrating everything
4. Communicating effectively

At TriStar Summit Medical Center, employees from various departments, along with department directors from the leadership team, defined and developed a list of our hospital values. We remembered them by using the acronym **I SERVE**. Our team agreed that living the values, rather than memorizing the values, was the most important thing we could do as leaders. The letters stood for:

I - Integrity
S - Selfless
E - Exceptional quality
R - Respect
V - Visionary
E - Excellence

A few years later, we revised our values statement to read "**I SERVE** *with pleasure*" in order to emphasize our commitment to providing exceptional customer service. Members of our team felt that the customer service at Chick-fil-A, an extremely successful fast-food restaurant chain, was outstanding. Chick-fil-A was the first fast-food restaurant that I knew of whose employees consistently replied, "My pleasure," after a customer said thank you. Brilliant idea! If teenagers could say "My pleasure," then so could we.

The Power of Calling People by Their First Name

Remembering and calling employees by their first names has a powerful influence on positive culture. Never underestimate it. One of the greatest sounds a person can hear is someone calling them by their first name. Dale Carnegie wrote about using first names in his best-selling book *How to Win Friends and Influence People*. Honor your teammates by using their first names. Learn their names if you haven't done so already.

When a leader calls people by their first names, they inject a jolt of positivity into the company culture. Employees appreciate it, and they never forget it.

Equally, asking employees to call you by your first name injects an additional jolt of positivity into the culture. I've never understood why some leaders expect staff to use Mr. or Ms. when addressing them. I cringe when I hear this. I've actually known of leaders who wished to be acknowledged as "president." Are you kidding me? Staff can't stand that display of ego, and I don't blame them.

I learned the value of using first names during my first job straight out of college at the public accounting firm KPMG. Bill Blaufuss, the firm's managing partner, asked all of us newbies to call him Bill. It sent a powerful message of equality that strongly impacted me throughout my career. I never forgot it, and I always asked our team to just call me Jeff. Everyone should feel equal because we *are* equal. We are all made in God's image. There is no place for a leader to feel special and above others by preferring to be called by their surname. Remember, everyone is equal.

Culture Starts at the Top

Developing and maintaining an encouraging and supportive culture starts with the leader. No doubt about it. As the leader, this is your responsibility. Own it. Having the right culture will make or break you as a leader. Many leaders believe that strategy development and implementation are most important. For them, culture doesn't rank very high. They say it does, but their actions prove otherwise. Those leaders care more about themselves and the bottom line than they do about their employees. Ironically, they underachieve and don't even know it.

Set the tone, and make culture a top priority. Actions speak louder than words. Develop a company culture that staff will love and fondly remember forever. And you might want to let them know that you own a pair of blue jeans!

Now, what about you?

1. Where does culture rank on your list of priorities?
2. Are you living the values of your organization?

#14

Celebrate Everything

"Remember to celebrate milestones
as you prepare for the road ahead."
— Nelson Mandela,
former president of South Africa

I had been with HCA for about five years when I interviewed for an open CEO position at another hospital in the company.

"Where does the hospital rank among all the hospitals in its latest employee satisfaction score?" I asked the senior leaders sitting across from me.

"It's not that good, but it's getting better," one of them replied.

"OK, but what is it?" I countered.

"We rank in the bottom 10 percent."

"Are you kidding me? Seriously? The bottom 10 percent out of more than three hundred hospitals?"

Low employee morale was one of the first major challenges that had to be addressed once I started. Many of the staff had been beaten down over the last few years by the former administration, who told them they were underachievers. Staff had no voice in the decisions that affected them. There was high turnover. Apathy had set in with most of those who stayed. Severe mistrust of hospital leadership was evident.

A Quick Win

One of the first actions of a successful new leader is to find a quick win—something to change or make better—and do it quickly. It shows that you are listening to your team and that you take action. You don't think about it for months. You do something about it now. Show your team that you care about them.

What could be the quick win here? Plenty of options existed because the hospital and campus had not been updated in years. Very drab and outdated on the inside. Outside, dead landscaping and a parking lot riddled with potholes and barely visible yellow parking stripes "welcomed" patients wishing to seek high-quality care, somewhat of an oxymoron.

The employee entrance hallway in the back of the hospital where we all parked was hideous. The wallpaper looked like it had been there since the hospital had opened eighteen years earlier. It was peeling in areas and riddled with stains . There were a number of holes in the wall and water spots on the ceiling. Walking through that hallway was depressing. It was a terrible way to start your day. It sent an unspoken message that senior leadership just didn't care, and neither should you.

The Light Bulb Moment

This was the quick win I was looking for: Upgrade the employee entrance hallway! With input from other staff throughout the hospital, it was totally upgraded and at minimal cost. Fresh paint, new wallcovering, new ceiling tiles, new flooring, motivational pictures on the wall, and an employee communication board. And we held a huge celebration with a ribbon cutting (along with the best junk food and cake ever) for the team. It was packed! In fact, it was so packed, I couldn't see all the employees who were there. They were lined up all the way down the upgraded hallway as well as the hallway to which it connected.

Country and classic rock music (my personal favorites) blared from the speakers. Smiles and laughter rang through the hallway. It was electrifying. Wow, I couldn't help but think that if our team got so enthused about upgrading a hallway, there was no telling how excited they were going to get when we accomplish larger goals. I was so jazzed! Our team had been starving for even a morsel of good news. They had no idea how many more celebrations would be coming their way in the future.

Over the years, the remodeled hallway became symbolic of "good news and celebrations." As weird as this may sound, all our future good news breaks and celebrations took place in that hallway. The staff loved it. It's what they wanted. Forget about the large classrooms that could easily accommodate everyone in a more comfortable setting. Our team preferred to be crowded in that upgraded hallway to celebrate (along with junk food and cake, of course). Upgrading that hallway was the quick win I desperately needed to jump-start our team, and its impact never ceased while I was there. In fact, we consistently ranked in the top 10 percent on our employee satisfaction scores from the day we celebrated our updated hallway. Simply amazing!

The Sound of Applause

Of all the celebrations that took place at all the hospitals I served, those that recognized employees and their accomplishments were the ones I cherished the most. Whether it was the annual employee awards dinner to honor staff for their years of service or our quarterly STARS (Superior Treatment and Royal Service) awards presented to staff, celebrations honoring and recognizing employees produced the greatest job satisfaction that I experienced as a CEO. It was priceless to see the smiles of those who were honored when their names were called. If family members happened to attend, their faces glowed with delight and appreciation. It moved me in such an emotional way. I, too, was so proud and happy for them. Their team was proud of them. And I'm sure they were a little proud of themselves, too. They deserved it.

Over time, I thought about the one thing that made these times of celebration and recognition so special for everyone. Sure, receiving a plaque, cash, or other gift was important. Having their picture hung on one of the hospital walls was significant. But what made it extraordinarily special was the sound of applause. Think about that for a moment—the sound of clapping hands, just for you. How many times in your life have you heard the sound of applause just for you? How did it make you feel? I dare say that not many of those being recognized had heard the sound of applause in quite some time. In fact, I bet many had not heard it in years, maybe decades. My guess is they couldn't remember what it felt like to hear such a loud ovation for no one else but them. Those celebrations were absolutely the most enjoyable and satisfying moments of my career. I loved our team.

A Reason to Celebrate

There's nothing like a good celebration at work, is there? We go at such a blistering pace that we sometimes fail to stop and celebrate successes achieved as a team. These can include departmental accomplishments, service line improvements, and plant expansions. Celebrations positively influence culture. It shows that the leader is acutely aware of the objectives or milestones others are achieving, and it's a powerful way to say thank you.

Celebrations are vital to a healthy organization. Find a reason to celebrate. It reinforces company values. Be purposeful to find opportunities big or small. The great leader seizes the opportunity to celebrate everything, even if it's just a simple upgrade to a worn-down employee entrance hallway.

Now, what about you?

1. When was the last time you recognized and celebrated a member of your team and they heard the sound of applause just for them?
2. What team goal, if accomplished, can you commit to celebrating in the next ninety days?

#15

Are You Listening?

"If speaking is silver, then listening is gold."
— Turkish Proverb

About a week after the world celebrated Y2K (Year 2000), I was sitting at the round table in my office while meeting with one of our department heads about her strategy to grow patient volume in her area of responsibility. Jean Seals was the director over a small, four-bed satellite emergency room (ER) and medical office building located in a small town about ten miles south of TriStar Southern Hills Medical Center. She was smart, a team player, and a highly respected member of her community. She was the ideal leader for that department.

I was not a patient listener. My motto: "If you can't write your message down on a yellow Post-it Note, then don't say it to me and try again." Active listening was not my forte. On top of that, I expected others to understand and comply with my communication style. I'm the boss, right? Looking back, that was quite shortsighted and arrogant of me. Major leadership flaw on my part.

Please get to the point, I thought. At the beginning of her presentation, I even interrupted and occasionally finished her sentences in order to speed up the meeting. I glanced at the clock strategically placed on a bookcase behind the table and cringed at the amount of time she was taking.

She had a vision and a plan to increase the number of patients seeking care at the ER, and ultimately to build a new hospital in her community. I didn't *hear* that message the first couple of times because I didn't truly *listen*. Sadly, I dismissed the idea of a new hospital. Once I listened patiently with a truly open mind a few years later, however, then I understood her plan. Although it was a bold vision, it had merit as an excellent long-term goal. Maybe a very long-term goal, but nevertheless, an excellent strategic goal. Growing ER patient volume by providing quality care, successfully marketing the ER, and recruiting specialty physicians to the campus could show the need for a new hospital in this community. Our team coined this the Expand the Border strategy. I liked it, but could it work?

The Art of Listening

For many leaders, active listening is not at the top of their skill set. In fact it's near the bottom. Why is this? It was definitely not one of my strengths. In fact, our associate administrator, a rising leader on our team at TriStar Summit Medical Center, said the following when I asked him about my listening skills: "You're the worst!" He was right. Active listening is a skill that I intentionally have to work on to this day. It can be such a positive characteristic for a leader if done properly.

Learn from the Best

One of the best leaders I know who has perfected the art of active listening is Joey Hogan, president of Covenant Logistics Group in Chattanooga, Tennessee. Joey and I grew up together in Chattanooga, went to school together from kindergarten through high school at Boyd-Buchanan, and roomed together in a dorm for all four years at Lipscomb University. We remain close friends today.

Joey possesses many leadership skills but active listening is one of his strongest. When you talk with him, he's completely focused on what you are telling him. He doesn't interrupt. His body language reflects that he's engaged. He maintains eye contact. He doesn't look at his watch or his cell phone. He's listening and thinking about what you are saying. He's in the zone. Laser focused.

Joey's secret sauce to active listening? He asks questions. He's curious. His questions are insightful. He's patient and respectful. His active listening skills are also a major component of his strong executive presence.

How Do You Improve?

Think about taking action on the following ideas in order to improve your active listening skills:

1. Ask questions.
2. Confirm with the person what you believe you have heard.
3. Don't listen with the intent to reply.
4. Develop patience and don't interrupt.
5. Remove all distractions such as your phone.

Expand the Border Strategy: Did It Work?

Not only did it work beautifully, it became one of our greatest success stories during my time at Southern Hills. A beautiful new hospital—TriStar StoneCrest Medical Center—opened in Smyrna, Tennessee, in November 2003. It remains one of the most successful hospitals in Middle Tennessee. I'm so glad that I finally listened.

Now, what about you?

1. How do you think your team would rate your listening skills?
2. What is the one thing you could do to improve your listening skills?

#16

Should I Stay or Should I Go?

"Always make decisions that prioritize your inner peace."
— Izey Victoria Odiase, self-care and
personal development advocate

"What should I do?" asked our chief operating officer. She was contemplating a job change outside the company and struggling with her decision. She was a terrific and talented leader on our team. No doubt she would achieve her goal of becoming a hospital CEO in the near future if she stayed with our company. However, she found the lure of a position in the corporate office of another hospital system extremely enticing.

"I can't answer that for you," I responded. I was kind but firm. "We've talked about it and debated it for the past two weeks. It's time for you to make a decision."

It was not the answer she wanted to hear. Pure silence as she looked at me. Nothing but crickets. *Say something, please.*

Anything. The silence is killing me.

Finally, I asked, "OK, let me ask you a couple of questions. Does the new job check off everything that's important for you to be personally happy and professionally challenged? Will it help you grow as a leader and position yourself for future advancement?"

"Yes, I really believe it does," she replied.

"There's your answer," I said with a smile. "As a boss and a mentor, go forward and make us all proud of you. Thank you for all you've done to make us a better team. You will be outstanding in your new role."

She smiled back. "Thank you. I'm taking the new position, and I promise you I will make you proud. I won't let you down."

Define What's Inside Your Boxes

Bill Rutherford, chief financial officer of HCA Healthcare, is both a friend and a mentor. I've always asked him for his advice and perspective on major decisions that I've faced in my professional journey. He is outstanding.

As I contemplated what I might do after retirement, one of the best pieces of advice Bill gave me was to clearly define what gets me excited about a job. I wanted to take some time off, but I knew that I still desired to do *something*. The problem was that I wasn't sure what that something was. He asked me to draw several boxes on a piece of paper. Inside each box, he challenged me to write down the critical must-haves for any job I might consider. In other words, I had to clearly define what went inside the boxes. I had to determine those few but critical satisfiers that got me excited and energized. Any job that I might consider had to satisfy what I wrote in each box.

After much thought and prayer, I defined what went into

my two boxes: First, I have to do something where there is human interaction, and second, I have to know that I'm making a difference in someone's life. By doing this exercise, I gained clarity on what I would do during the next season of my life.

Key Questions to Ask Yourself

Have you ever gotten the itch to do something new? The itch that gnaws at you and doesn't seem to go away? Is it time to look for a new job?

Ask yourself the following questions to help determine if it's time to scratch the itch:

1. Have I defined my boxes?
2. What boxes are unchecked in my current job?
3. Can I reinvent my current role in order to check off the boxes?
4. Are there other jobs inside the organization that excite me?
5. Am I leaving my job because of my boss or because I want to do something else?
6. What must I learn and do to position myself for advancement within the company?
7. Am I truly ready to leave my team and take on the unknowns of a new job?

Everyone wants to be wanted. You are filled with euphoria and confidence when another company or department within your current company wants you to join their team. It validates that you are very good at what you do. In fact, the new company or department perceives that you can add value to their team, and they want you. That feeling is so powerful. Sometimes it's so powerful that it can cloud your judgment if it's not kept in check. Remember, "the grass isn't always greener on the other side of the fence." Whoever first said that was a genius.

Before You Accept

How do you know if you should accept a new job offer? It's a huge decision in your professional journey. It might possibly be a "fork in the road" for you. Before accepting, ask yourself the following the questions:

1. Does the new job check off all my boxes?
2. Does it excite, challenge, and energize me?
3. Do I like and respect my future boss?
4. Is the culture of the new company or department what I want?
5. How will the new job affect my family?
6. Will this job allow me to grow and position myself for future advancement?
7. Is the compensation fair and acceptable?

If you answer yes to the questions above, consider the job. But if you answer no to any of the questions, then you have to challenge yourself on whether this is the right job for you. I've coached clients after they've accepted and started a new job but didn't ask themselves the questions above. They are unhappy and kick themselves for leaving their previous roles. Unfortunately, the grass wasn't greener on the other side of the fence. The first question they ask me: "Now what?" Good question. You tell me.

Check Off the Boxes

Take the time to draw and fill in the boxes. Let your answers guide you to the best decision. The timing might not be right to take on a new job. Nonetheless, you've taken action to evaluate what's important to you and what boxes must be checked off before you seriously consider the job.

She Checked Off the Boxes

Melissa Waddey, our COO who accepted the new job, was very successful at her new company. She "checked off the boxes" before she made her decision. I was extremely proud of her. Although she passed away at a young age, she positively impacted the lives of so many people in such a short period of time. It was an honor and a privilege to have had the opportunity to work with her.

Now, what about you?

1. Have you defined what's inside your boxes?
2. What questions do you ask yourself before accepting a promotion or new position?

17

The One Thing You Have That Everybody Wants

"Either run the day or the day runs you."
— Jim Rohn, entrepreneur and author

I kept looking at my watch, silently pleading for this dull 7:00 a.m. meeting at TriStar Summit Medical Center to end. *Why am I even here?* I was not participating other than looking at the agenda in front of me and checking off each item discussed with my pen. Tick-tock, tick-tock, tick-tock. All I could think about were the rest of the meetings on my calendar for the day. It was going to be one of those days—I could just sense it.

As soon as this "thrilling" meeting was over, I rushed to one of the classrooms to conduct the first of five employee open meetings for the day. I loved these meetings with our staff. Peggy Peeler, our executive assistant, had prepared the Power-Point presentation and gave me the clicker when I walked in. I immediately welcomed everyone and began the presentation.

Great questions, as always, from our team. My hope was that they would remember just a few of the updates and feel like they knew where we stood and where we were headed as a hospital and as a team. However, the day was packed and I didn't have the time to chat much after the meeting. *Hate it, but I have to go.* My iPhone vibrated, first text of the day. *Oh, great.*

I then began walking quickly throughout the hospital and talked with employees and physicians. I'm a fast walker by nature. Needed to hurry. Someone pinged me with another text. *Good grief.* No time to look. I just kept walking.

At 9:55 a.m., the next employee open meeting was scheduled to start in five minutes. A teammate told me about a problem as I briskly walked to the meeting. I really didn't have time to listen. *Please, just quickly state the problem and your recommendation to solve it. I'm begging you—you are killing me with so many details!* Terrible active listening on my part, I know.

I attended a couple of additional meetings sandwiched between the second and third employee open meetings. I sorted emails on my phone every chance I got. Read, respond, swipe, delete—that was the plan.

I left the hospital and drove to our Summit Outpatient Services Building to deliver the next employee open meeting presentation to our staff who worked off campus. They couldn't attend the meetings at the hospital due to their busy schedules. Meeting at their building was a great idea they had suggested a few years earlier.

My Stomach's Growling

No time for lunch that day except for a Diet Coke and a candy bar. Wonder what caused my love handles to grow—that certainly didn't help.

When I returned, I learned that a member of our division office had placed a conference call on my calendar for later that day. *Seriously? Today?* My schedule was adjusted to accommodate this unexpected call. A number of folks were scheduled to meet with me that day. I hate rescheduling or canceling meetings, even if it's unavoidable, but a conference call from the division office trumped any other meeting.

After another meeting, I sat down and waited for the conference call to begin. I knocked out more emails as fast as I could. I scanned the list of senders to see if any of them were above me on the organization chart. Lo and behold, there happened to be one, and the subject line read: "URGENT!" *How did I miss this one?* The email looked like it was just to me—that was never a good sign. I read it and responded immediately. My phone vibrated again, another text. I hoped that it didn't start with the word "URGENT!"

The rest of the day was just as busy as it started. Finally, it was over. Time to go home and see my family. I was mentally and physically exhausted. I was glad I had a thirty-minute commute just to have some time to myself to decompress. Almost every day on the drive home, I would say to myself, "I absolutely love my job, and I can't believe I get paid to do this!" There were a few days, however, that I would say, "I don't get paid nearly enough for what I went through today." That day was definitely one of the latter.

What's the One Thing?

Have you ever had a day like that? I'm sure you have. In fact, I'm sure you've had lots of them. I learned early on that there was one thing I had that everyone wanted: My time. Everyone wants your time. Your work, family, church, friends, and community want your time. Your time is the scarcest and most finite resource you have, and everyone wants a slice of it. Leaders must decide where to put their time and energy in order to maximize their effectiveness.

The challenge is how to adequately divide your time among those competing for it while still accomplishing the goals and actions you have set for yourself. We have only twenty-four hours in a day—that's it. Therefore, in order to *have* time, you must *create* time by *saving* time wherever possible.

How Do You Do It?

There are a number of strategies you can implement to help you create time by saving time. Here are a few:

1. Say no to unimportant meetings and committees.
2. Block off time on your calendar to focus on top priorities.
3. Resist constantly checking your emails.
4. Turn off notifications on your phone.
5. Eliminate or limit social media.

Choose one nugget from above and implement it today. Write it down and commit to it. Try it for at least twenty-one consecutive days in order to evaluate its effectiveness. See what happens. You just might find you have created some time. Remember, it's the one thing you have that everybody wants, including you.

Now, what about you?

1. How do you prioritize your time to focus on what's most important?
2. What can you do to feel more comfortable saying no to unimportant meetings and committees?

#18

Why Am I Still Talking?

"Being self-aware is not the absence of mistakes,
but the ability to learn and correct them."
— Daniel Chidiac, author,
Who Says You Can't? You Do

We were about two hours into our monthly meeting between hospital CEOs and senior division leadership. No restroom break—strictly business. My bladder was about to burst, but I didn't leave because I didn't want to miss anything. The meeting was intense. You could see the stress on everyone's face, including mine. As a collective group of hospitals, we had missed our budgeted expectations for the fourth consecutive quarter. No one was happy.

There were multiple factors that contributed to the disappointing results. It was mid-2009, and the Great Recession gripped the country. Sure, the economy affected us but that wasn't the sole reason for our dismal results. It wasn't any one person's fault. We had strong and talented hospital CEOs. But we had missed our budget again as a division, and the pressure was on to turn it around—and quickly. I felt the tension like everyone else in the room. As hospital CEOs and senior division leadership, winning was in our DNA. Losing was gut-wrenching. I hate to lose almost as much as I love to win, and we were losing the game.

I Didn't See This Coming

Senior division leadership brought up a subject that wasn't on the agenda we'd received prior to the meeting. I quickly realized that the subject pertained solely to me, as the leaders fired multiple questions at me and none at my colleagues. I felt attacked. I was embarrassed because it was happening in front of my peers rather than privately. However, it was my responsibility to maintain my composure and to treat those in authority with respect. Unfortunately, I did neither.

The veins in my neck popped out. My blood boiled. My face became beet red as I tried to hold back. And then, I got angry. I lost my cool. Not good. My voice got louder. I lashed back at a senior division leader disrespectfully. I defended myself but in an unprofessional manner. The more I talked, the worse it got.

In my head, a little voice repeatedly asked, *Why am I still talking?* Sadly, I didn't listen to my inner voice the first time. Nor the second or third time. Then it hit me squarely in the forehead: shut up and retreat. Point made but damage done. What was I thinking?

Where Was My Self-Awareness?

Self-awareness is a critical component of leadership that many people lack. It was certainly missing in my leadership from time to time. It is a skill that is underdeveloped and overlooked by most leaders. Why is that?

Leaders must reflect on their actions and words. They must read and interpret the situation correctly. Egos must be held in check. Leaders must control the words they say and the tone in which they are said. Leaders have to seriously ask themselves, "Could I have handled myself in a more appropriate and professional manner?" Honest self-reflection is necessary. Your conclusion might sting, but you will have identified an area of personal growth.

Three Game-changing Questions

Without a doubt, the absolute best advice to increase self-awareness and one's response to others came from Craig Ferguson, a comedian and TV personality. His take was quoted in an article in *Inc.* magazine.[2] In stressful situations, he said that he asked himself three questions:

1. Does this need to be said?
2. Does this need to be said by me?
3. Does this need to be said by me right now?

Wow, this is pure gold! I wish I had known about these three questions while I was a CEO. Think about how answering these questions before responding to someone could positively influence your words, your timing, and your results. Sometimes some things just don't need to be said. There is no value or gain to be had. Your response might feel satisfying in the moment, but it causes damage in the long run. Strong self-control is a virtue.

---

2   Justin Bariso, "Why Emotionally Intelligent Minds Embrace the 3-Question Rule," *Inc.*, April 20, 2021, https://www.inc.com/justin-bariso/why-emotionally-intelligent-minds-embrace-3-question-rule.html.

On the other hand, some things need to be said, just not by you. Don't take the bait. Don't own the problem if it's not yours. Let the other person say it. Why should you respond on behalf of someone else, especially if it's controversial? Take a deep breath. Bite your lip if you have to. Do whatever it takes to not respond.

Finally, some things need to be said, and they need to be said by you, but they don't need to be said right now. Timing is everything. Strong self-awareness assists in determining the right timing. How often have you reflected on a conversation and realized that your timing was bad? Good timing is a skill that effective leaders possess. They have a sense of when to talk and when to be quiet. They understand that some things can be better achieved if they don't respond in the moment but defer to meeting in a private setting.

Self-reflection Time

I learned several lessons in that meeting with senior leadership. First, understand that stressful situations sometimes cause people to say things they might regret. That was certainly the case for me. Second, improve self-awareness in meetings by asking yourself the three questions before you respond. Finally, be professional enough to reflect on your behavior and to make amends when needed.

I put together a follow-up meeting with the senior division leader with whom I had the confrontation at the meeting with CEOs. I apologized for my actions. He deserved more respect than I gave him at the meeting. He is a class act and was over it by the time we talked. I respected him even more after we met. We remain friends today.

I've coached a number of executives on how to improve their self-awareness and to ask themselves the three questions before responding. Invariably, they tell me that it is one of the most valuable pieces of advice that they picked up during the entire coaching engagement.

When you're about to respond to a question that tweaks you in some way, take a nanosecond and ask yourself the three self-awareness questions before, or if, you respond. Let your answers lead you to the correct decision. The last thing you want to hear is that inner voice asking, "Why am I still talking?"

Now, what about you?

1. How often do you reflect on how you handled certain situations?
2. How can you make it a habit to ask yourself the three game-changing questions?

#19

The Look

"The greatest of faults is to be conscious of none."
— Thomas Carlyle, British historian

The conversation between Emily, our teenage daughter, and me was not going in the right direction as we sat at the dinner table. She was tired, I was tired, and we were both hungry. Deadly combination.

"Mama, Daddy just gave me 'the look'!" Emily said to Jennifer, who was standing next to the stove in the kitchen. A slight grin appeared on Emily's face as she looked at me. *Enlisting others to divert attention from the conversation— well played*, I thought.

Ashleigh, who was home from college, didn't hesitate to jump right in. She somewhat laughingly said, "Oh, no. You never want to get 'the look' from Daddy." Emily's plan was working. It was now two against one.

"I know 'the look'," replied Jennifer, "and I've been on the receiving end of it many times. It's not pretty." Emily's smile widened.

"What look?" I replied, my eyes squinted and my face distorted with puzzlement. "I have no idea what you're talking about." At that moment, I knew it was now three against one. Emily won.

They proceeded to explain that I occasionally give people a certain look whenever I perceive they are disagreeing with me, not understanding me, or taking too much time to make their point. "No way that I do this," I argued. Secretly, I wondered if they were somehow right and I was wrong. It just can't be.

I Just Have to Know

I decided to investigate my family's allegation the next morning at the hospital. During a break between meetings, Peggy Peeler, the best executive assistant I ever worked with, came into my office to ask a question. As she was walking out, I asked, "Peggy, do I sometimes give people a certain look while I'm talking with them? My family says that I give others a demeaning look at times. Is this true?" Nothing like putting the person you rely on the most while at work on the spot.

Peggy stopped walking. She thought for a few seconds, then hesitantly but kindly confirmed what my family had said the night before: "I hate to tell you this, but you do give people a certain look at times." She smiled and said everyone at the hospital called it "The Look." *Oh, no, my family was right and I was wrong.*

Leadership Blind Spots

I had no idea that I had this leadership blind spot. Had my family not told me about it, I might never have known. You can't blame those who work with you for not telling you—who wants to tell the boss about one of their blind spots? How crazy was it that I gave such a negative, disgusted look to others and didn't even know it?

Every leader has blind spots. You're kidding yourself if you think you don't have any. Blind spots hold back our effectiveness. They also distort how we perceive ourselves compared to the reality of how others actually see us. Leaders who don't address and eliminate their blind spots will underachieve in the long run. Sad thing is that they will never know that they could have been better.

How to Identify Blind Spots

If you want to pinpoint your leadership blind spots, I believe that engaging in a 360-degree assessment is the best tool to do this. This assessment asks for feedback from your boss, peers, subordinates, yourself, and others within the organization who observe your leadership behaviors. The assessment will display the gap, if any, between how the observers you selected rate your leadership skills compare to how you rate yourself. You can then see the skills in which you excel and those that have room for improvement.

You have to allow yourself to be vulnerable and open to feedback. It can sting a bit. Denial might creep in but don't allow it. The feedback is a blessing, as it identifies your blind spots. You now know the obstacles that you must overcome to maximize your leadership potential.

There are numerous books about leadership blind spots and how to overcome them. The book I recommend to my executive coaching clients is *What Got You Here Won't Get You There* by Marshall Goldsmith. It is outstanding. The author identifies and discusses a number of leadership blind spots in the book. I was guilty of many of them, and I had no idea.

Find Someone Who Will Tell You Like It Is

Walt Leaver, our pulpit minister at Brentwood Hills Church of Christ in Nashville, may be the best storyteller that I've ever heard. He has a magical ability of making a meaningful point while telling a captivating story. The audience is enthralled while he speaks, and they hang onto his every word. He's amazing.

He told a story about how his mother, Anne Leaver, gave him some feedback. Miss Anne was one of the sweetest people God has ever placed on this earth. Before she gave Walt this feedback, she prefaced it with one of the greatest introductory sentences for constructive criticism of all time: "Walt, I'm the only person in this world who loves you enough to tell you this." Boom! Walt talked about how he perked up and braced himself for what was about to come. What a blessing it was for Walt to have someone who would tell him like it really is. Wouldn't it be nice if all of us had someone like that, whether in or outside of work?

Leadership blind spots are real. You can either identify and address them or live in denial. Consider taking action by investing in a Leadership 360 Assessment or reading a book on leadership blind spots. Even better, can you find a "Miss Anne" in your world who can "tell you like it really is"? Discover and eliminate blind spots like "The Look." Your team will thank you!

Now, what about you?

1. How have you solicited feedback from others to help you identify your blind spots?
2. What have you done to overcome them?

20

Igniting Teamwork

> "Alone, we can do so little.
> Together we can do so much more."
> — Helen Keller

"The winner of the Leadership Team MVP Award, as voted on by your peers, is . . . Scott Vogt!" I shouted. The hospital department directors went wild! Everyone in the room cheered and clapped, including Scott's wife and children, who had been invited to the celebration. The directors gave him a standing ovation. Scott was stunned. You could read it all over his face as he slowly stood up from his chair.

As he walked to the head table to accept the award, his eyes were moist. His chin quivered slightly. Then, something happened that I hadn't witnessed in the entire year since I hired him: He was *speechless*. I was shocked. Here's a leader to whom I once gave constructive feedback because he talked way too much and listened way too little, but in this moment, he literally could not utter a single word. Simply amazing.

Why did Scott, our new director of plant operations, win

this award? What was it about him that drove his peers to vote him MVP of our team? I was pretty sure I knew the reason, but I asked a number of department heads why they felt Scott deserved the award. They all said the same thing: "He's a team player."

Scott was the model team player when we worked together in 1996 at Fairview Park Hospital in Dublin, Georgia. He helped his teammates in whatever ways they needed. He did the same thing for the staff in the departments he supervised. There wasn't an assignment that he didn't gladly take on. He worked some crazy hours at the beginning in order to help me get the hospital's appearance back to where it should be. He took pride in his work. His dedication motivated others to set and achieve higher standards. Plainly stated, he put the team before himself.

The Killer Phrase

Anyone who believes in the value and reward of teamwork absolutely despises hearing this certain phrase. It's like a sucker punch to the gut. It's the phrase that can stop all progress toward accomplishing a team goal. It's baffling and confusing to a team player. It's a selfish excuse not to help.

The killer phrase that destroys teamwork? It's when an uncommitted teammate replies, "It's not my job."

This phrase has caused so many teams to stumble and flounder. It gouges creativity and *esprit de corps*. That selfish attitude allows problems to remain unsolved. It can cause backbiting and disunity. And the reason? The employee just doesn't care. Apathetic employees are only concerned for themselves. They have no idea what it feels like to successfully accomplish a team goal by working together. They rob themselves and others of this euphoric feeling of accomplishment.

Team players realize that it's everyone's job to work together to achieve common goals and make the organization or department better.

The Powerful Phrase

There's just something special about those on a team who have vision and commitment. They know there are obstacles that must be overcome in order to achieve the goal. They might not have an answer to the problem yet, but they know there's one out there. They thrive on the sense of accomplishment in "cracking the nut" and solving the problem. They are overwhelmingly committed to finding a solution through teamwork.

The powerful phrase that ignites teamwork: "We will either find a way, or make one." This quote is attributed to Hannibal, a Carthaginian military general, who spoke the phrase while crossing the Alps on elephants during the Second Punic War, approximately 218 BC.

Boom! A jolt of adrenaline rushes through one's body when a member of the team voices such a phrase. The look of excitement and confidence beams on each teammate's face. They know, somehow, it can be done. They have tasted the intoxicating nectar of accomplishment in the past when they achieved a goal as a team. There is nothing like it! They will do whatever it takes to experience that natural high of achievement again and again.

Indeed, Hannibal and his generals found a way to cross the Alps. Faced with insurmountable obstacles, they figured it out. Only through teamwork could something of this magnitude have been achieved. It started with vision and commitment.

The same is true with those teammates who don't stop until they find a solution. There is a role for everyone on the team. Roles may change as different problems confront the team over time. However, these teammates see the vision and are committed to working together to find a solution.

Crossing the Alps Today

My belief is that you're already a "We will find a way" type of leader. Otherwise, you wouldn't be investing your time into reading this book. Here's the big question: Do those on your team share the same attitude, vision, and commitment that you do? Be extremely honest with yourself on this one. Sometimes, as much as we want to answer yes to the question, the truthful answer is no. If that's the case, then you have the option to either manage them up or move them out. A neutral position doesn't exist. There's no seat on the bus for someone with an "It's not my job" attitude. Remember, your success as a leader is directly dependent on the success of your team.

Scott Vogt was "Hannibal-like." His commitment to teamwork helped us find ways to overcome obstacles in order to achieve success. I challenge you to ignite teamwork and lead your team "across the Alps" the next time a challenging problem confronts the team. Be a leader like Hannibal, a leader like Scott.

Now, what about you?

1. What can you do to ignite teamwork to achieve higher goals?
2. What actions do you take to reinforce teamwork over individual performance?

21

Anticipate the Unexpected

"Remember this: Anticipation is the ultimate power.
Losers react. Winners anticipate."
— Tony Robbins, author and motivational speaker

While I was CEO at TriStar Summit Medical Center, I had the opportunity to work with several chairpersons of our board of trustees over the years. At our bimonthly meeting, one particular chairperson was moving through the agenda at a pretty good clip. Nothing was out of the ordinary so far. The board members were all in good moods that morning. The table had the usual white tablecloth along with excellent breakfast food. The setting was perfect, and the meeting was going as planned.

Only one problem: A potentially controversial proposal near the bottom of the agenda had not yet been discussed. It was crucial that it be passed in order to support the hospital's growth plan. However, it was risky. In fact, it contained so much risk that it could either be viewed as one of the best decisions I ever made or one of the worst.

For various reasons, the strategic growth plan of the hospital no longer aligned with the growth plan of one physician group with whom we had a contractual relationship. The physicians were excellent doctors; however, neither side agreed on the role and expectations of how their practice would support the hospital's strategic plan. After a year of trying to resolve our differences and find middle ground, it became obvious that it was time to part ways. No hard feelings, at least from my perspective. It was just time. Actually, it was past time.

I anticipated, as best as I could, the reactions of all stakeholders to this move. I had intentionally updated the board throughout the year on the problems we consistently encountered with this group, as well as our inability to resolve our differences. I recommended that we sever the agreement with the physician group. The result? The board unanimously approved the recommendation. I was relieved, but communicating our decision to the physician group would most likely be explosive. No one likes to be told that their services are no longer needed.

I Didn't See That Coming

I anticipated potential fallout with other members of the medical staff once the decision became public. In order to combat this, I had briefed multiple physician leaders, as well as a number of informal group leaders, on what was about to happen. I had asked for their input—they knew the plan and supported the change. I had kept my boss informed along the way and had his support. I had informed the hospital leadership team of the change in order for them to be ready to manage any problems that might arise. I had arranged a face-to-face meeting for the following day with the physician group's leader to communicate the board's decision. We were ready to execute the plan. So far, so good—or so I thought.

Once the board meeting was over, I saw the chairperson remove the agenda and secretively slip it into his pocket as he walked out. Our policy was that no documents were to leave the boardroom. Although he had voted in favor of the change, I knew this was not going to be good. My gut said that he was going to tell the group himself, and in all likelihood, take no responsibility and blame the hospital. It most likely would be presented that administration (aka me) had made the decision to terminate the contract. I uttered a phrase I hate to say: "I didn't see that coming."

I conferred with Tom Ozburn, our COO at the time, on the best course of action given this unforeseen move. We both quickly agreed: Alter the plan and find one of the leaders of the physician group right away, and give that physician written notice that the contract was being terminated. We needed to control the messaging, not the board chairperson. It might or might not reduce the fallout, but better to be proactive.

The Outcome

The aftermath of the announcement to the physician group was correctly predicted: Extreme anger and disruption. I took a number of "knives to the back" over the next month or so, but I held my ground. Physician leaders stood with us. It was the right move. As the leader, it was my job to make the call even though I knew in the short run that I would take some incredible heat.

Within six months, the decision proved to be the right one for both the physician group and the hospital. Both parties moved on with their strategic plans and thrived over the long term. Although some of the physician group's older members had some hard feelings, the majority of the physicians agreed that the decision benefited them as well as the hospital.

Taillights

Great leaders *anticipate* the unexpected, they don't just expect the unexpected. To me, one takes action and the other does not. As an example, consider stop-and-go traffic on the interstate. Average drivers look at the taillights on the car in front of them to decide whether to accelerate, decelerate, or brake. Sometimes they wreck. Great drivers, however, look at the taillights on the cars ahead of the car in front of them. It helps them anticipate what the car ahead of them will do, and reduces the risk of a wreck.

The same can be said for leaders and their ability to anticipate rather than react. Average leaders just look at what information is in front of them and sometimes make rushed and reactionary decisions. On the other hand, great leaders anticipate the unexpected by looking ahead and taking in information that will give them more time to make the correct decision.

Anticipate and Take Action

Many different people have said, "Expect the unexpected." No doubt that this is a true statement. However, I believe "Anticipate the unexpected" is the better saying for great leaders. It means taking action on the front end. Plus, it puts the leader in the *driver's* seat. Which car's taillights are you watching?

Now, what about you?

1. What are the benefits of anticipating the unexpected?
2. How can you improve your ability to anticipate the reactions of others?

#22

Balancing Passion
with Compassion

"Compassion is passion with a heart."
— Unknown

The interview schedule for nurses applying for our division's chief nursing officer development program was set. I had been asked to join several of my colleagues from other HCA sister hospitals in Nashville to participate in group interviews with each candidate. The program was a terrific opportunity for nurses wishing to grow their leadership skills and advance in their careers. Like most development programs, the number of candidates far exceeded the number of open slots. Competition was keen, and nailing the group interview was critical for each candidate during the selection process.

The last candidate on the schedule had a very impressive resume. She had relevant experience, had been recently promoted, and possessed a strong educational background. On paper, she looked solid.

When asked to describe her management style, the applicant answered somewhat smugly. "I always make the budget, never miss. I push my team hard to achieve results. In fact, I set stretch goals that are virtually impossible to meet so that my staff works even harder to get great results."

"What have you done to improve your patient satisfaction scores?" an interviewer asked.

"If I see or hear about anyone on my team not doing a good job, I pull them into my office and give them a lecture, if you know what I mean. No excuses allowed. I won't put up with any whining," she boasted.

Ouch, now that's harsh! I wonder if she allows them to talk and give their side of the story? I began to have a bad feeling about this candidate. I sensed that she saw everything in black or white, and that no gray zone existed. That narrow viewpoint in a leader is scary to me. Life is full of gray.

I thought for a moment, then I asked her, "I hear *passion* in your answers about achieving results, but do you have an example of a time you showed *compassion* as a leader?"

She paused, looking slightly shocked, then said, "Of course. One of my nurses had a child get sick last week, so I let her go home an hour early."

Wow, that's pretty big of you—a whole hour. Perhaps a "stretch goal" for you?

Needless to say, this candidate did not get selected for the program. All the members of the interviewing group came to the same conclusion: She lacks compassion, doesn't listen, and loves control. She's not the kind of leader we're looking for.

The Importance of
Passion and Compassion

Leaders must have passion and compassion to excel. You cannot have one without the other to be truly successful. It's commendable to see leaders passionate for results who do whatever it takes to win. That's all good if kept in check in a healthy way. However, *compassion* has to be there in order to balance the passion. Compassion flows from the heart, and others see it in the words we say and the actions that we take.

Leaders who possess and show compassion connect with others on a deeper level, whether it's those they lead or the customers they serve. This connection develops trust, which is the cornerstone of winning teamwork. Trust moves the team forward. Compassion is the fuel that drives the creation and formation of trust.

Compassion compels leaders to pause, evaluate, and then proceed. In other words, compassion in decision-making can cause leaders to reflect on and consider the ramifications of their decisions. What might look like an easy solution to a problem could have a significantly negative impact on other people. Compassion causes leaders to evaluate other options to resolve issues. Subsequently, they make better decisions.

Compassionate leaders are more respected, and members of their team perceive them to be better, more capable leaders, which results in increased loyalty. Staff are more apt to follow a leader who displays compassion.

A Compassionate Leader

President Abraham Lincoln has consistently ranked as one of America's greatest presidents by different polls and groups throughout the years. Why has he been so respected and revered as a leader? Was it because of the difficult circumstances of our country during the time he led? Was it because of his passion to achieve great success? Possibly. However, I believe it was his *compassion* for others that made him an extraordinary leader. He never wavered in his true belief that all people are created equal. Every action he took supported this belief. It wasn't easy, but he successfully kept our country together. He is a prime example of a leader who balanced passion with compassion in an extraordinary way.

Now, what about you?

1. How would your team answer if they were asked whether or not you lead with compassion?
2. What example can you pass along to your team where compassion influenced a major decision you made?

23

Making Tough Decisions Is Part of the Job

"The truth of the matter is that you always know
the right thing to do. The hard part is doing it."
— General Norman Schwarzkopf, former commander,
Operation Desert Storm

Most hospital CEOs relocate several times through-out their careers in order to advance and lead larger hospitals. I was no exception. The excitement and rush of adrenaline to arrive on day one as the new CEO was such a euphoric feeling. Though obstacles and challenges awaited, the thrill of assembling a team, defining vision, establish-ing relationships, setting team goals, and achieving positive results far exceeded the difficulties I would encounter along the way.

Early in my career I was appointed CEO of a hospital in middle Georgia. There were a number of challenges confront-ing me when I arrived: Financial performance was dismal, physician relations had declined significantly, and patient volumes had dropped appreciably. Employees were nervous because they feared an imminent reduction in force. The former CEO, a genuinely nice person, had resigned abruptly. It might not have been the best of situations, but it provided me with an opportunity to lead a larger hospital and advance within the company. I gladly accepted the challenge.

The Situation

The former CEO had made the decision to recruit five new family practice doctors at the same time in order to form a large physician group. All five physicians were completing their residencies, which meant they had never been in private practice and didn't know how to start and grow a practice. Also, this was the first time that the hospital had entered into an employment contract with physicians. The physicians in the current family practice group were furious. They had been mostly loyal to the hospital for years, but their relationship with hospital leadership had deteriorated tremendously.

The Problems

The five physicians still finishing their residencies had no idea how to build their patient volume. The operational cost to employ five physicians for a start-up practice was staggering—and to make matters worse, unbudgeted. There was not enough office space for their practice, so the hospital had committed to building them a new, free-standing office building for approximately $1 million. And the existing primary care physician group, furious about the perceived competition, threatened to refer 100 percent of their patients to a competing hospital.

The Options

Terminate the recruiting agreement and employment contract with the five new physicians before they came on board. Renegotiate the recruiting agreement with the new group in order to reduce significant start-up costs. Or honor the commitment to the new group but risk losing a substantial number of patients from the existing family practice group.

The Decision

I chose to honor the commitment the previous hospital CEO had made to the new group of doctors. It was the right thing to do. What message would I send to others if I didn't honor the promise made to these doctors? Sure, I understood the risk. Not everyone on the medical staff was going to be happy with my call, especially the veteran group of primary care physicians. The cost would be a significant hit to the financials at the beginning, but there was considerable upside for the future if the group was successful. The community would win because there were not enough primary care doctors to serve the growing population.

The Outcome

The new group came in on fire and quickly established a thriving practice. They seemed to have a point to prove. The volume of patients utilizing the hospital increased—by a lot. Operational results improved radically. Employees forgot about possible layoffs because they got busier. In fact, we had to hire additional staff to handle the increased patient volume. The specialty physicians were pleased with the decision because they got busier, too. As for the existing group of primary care physicians who had been upset about my decision, they profoundly disliked me until the day I left town. In fact, I was surprised they didn't show up to help load the moving van!

Tough Decisions Define You as a Leader

If you desire to be a leader, then know that making tough decisions is part of the job. They won't earn you a 100 percent approval rating from those you lead or those affected by your decisions. Many aspiring leaders believe the fallacy that they will be liked, even beloved, by their followers or subordinates. This couldn't be further from the truth. Addressing and making tough decisions define you; they don't always endear you.

Obstacles and challenges confront all leaders. Welcome the opportunity to take them head on. Making tough decisions is just part of the job. I never saw "must make tough decisions" written in any job description, but that's what a leader gets paid to do. Get used to it. Some you get right, some you get wrong. It's just a part of leadership. Do your homework, make and implement the decision, and move on. Another obstacle is just around the corner in your leadership journey.

Now, what about you?

1. What can you do to make decisions in a more timely manner?
2. What can you do to overcome the need to be liked by everyone?

#24

Want to be Promoted?
Be a High Achiever

"Mediocre people don't like high achievers,
and high achievers don't like mediocre people."
— Nick Saban, head football coach,
University of Alabama

His current boss was enthusiastic and said he was "talented and ready to be promoted." Our division president described him as a "diamond in the rough who just needed a bit of polishing." A peer of mine said, "He has potential." So which was it?

I wanted a high achiever to fill our open COO position at TriStar Summit Medical Center, the last hospital I led in my hospital administration career. The previous COO had been promoted to CEO at a hospital in Florida. I loved seeing COOs with whom I worked be promoted to CEOs. I wanted the streak to continue.

I wasn't sure that I wanted a candidate with only

"potential." Darrell Royal, the legendary former head football coach at the University of Texas, once said, "Potential means you just ain't done it yet." I wanted a proven winner who was a high achiever. The recommendations varied. Again, which one was right?

He interviewed for the open position. I had to determine whether he was a high achiever and whether he could fit within the system I liked to lead. You would work very hard, I would throw a lot at you so that you could learn and test your limits, but you would be ready to be a successful CEO when your number was called.

So did he get the job? Stay tuned.

High Achievers Win

Throughout my career as a CEO, I mentored a number of leaders on my teams on how to position themselves for their next promotion. Today, I coach many clients on how to do the same thing. From my perspective, it hasn't really changed much over the years. High achievers move up, while mediocre leaders either turn it around or move out. Sure, company politics can get in the way at times, but this is usually not the norm. It's the high achievers who triumph. They outperform others, win, and move up, though not always in the time frame they desire. Regardless, high achievers succeed most often.

Attributes of High Achievers

High achievers have the following attributes:

1. **They excel in their current role.** They produce results and exceed expectations. They meet deadlines. They're not late for meetings or conference calls, whether virtual or in person. They're team players

and good communicators.

2. **They take on additional responsibility.** They ask their supervisor for more tasks to undertake. They say yes to projects their boss wishes to delegate. They have an insatiable hunger to learn.

3. **They recognize the importance of KYBBOYBB (Keep Your Boss's Boss Off Your Boss's Back).** High achievers protect their boss's back. They do this by performing their jobs well and by making sure that their boss's boss is not worried about the areas for which they are accountable. They want their boss to succeed and to never be caught off guard.

4. **They have outstanding executive presence.** They possess an appropriate amount of self-confidence and gravitas. They know how to effectively communicate with others.

5. **They develop and grow their internal and external networks.** Networking allows high achievers to develop strategic relationships. Some of these relationships might lead to unknown opportunities. Such connections allow them to explore what other positions might be out there. Successful leaders expand their internal network by including colleagues who work in different areas of the company. They expand their external network by developing relationships outside their company, such as those from similar professional organizations, places of worship, or nonprofits at which they volunteer. High achievers value and understand the importance of having both networks.

Tenure Versus Results

I've seen some people within organizations make a common but false assumption. For some reason, they believe that their boss or their company owes them the new role or promotion that they are seeking. They illogically reason that they deserve the position because they have been with the company longer than other candidates. They believe that "tenure trumps results." This is just not true. It's all about hiring the absolute best person for the job, a leader who can achieve future success.

Let me be frank—the organization doesn't owe anyone a promotion. It must be earned. Internal leaders must position themselves for future promotions. There might be better external candidates who should be considered. It's the organization's responsibility to hire the best candidate for the job. Please don't get caught up in this false assumption that tenure trumps results.

Did He Get the Job?

He got the job. I knew immediately when I interviewed Tom Ozburn that he was the leader I wanted. Other hospital and physician leaders felt the same way. During his time at Summit, he accomplished so much in the areas of hospital operations, patient growth, and employee engagement. One of his greatest accomplishments was forming our Spiritual Committee, one that continues to excel to this day. He has continued to advance his career and currently serves as an HCA market president. He is a high achiever, and I'm very proud of him.

Promotions don't come along every day. Be a high achiever. Seek to emulate the attributes of high performers and position yourself as the best candidate for your desired promotion.

Now, what about you?

1. What can you consistently do to convince others that you are a high achiever?
2. How do you practice KYBBOYBB?

#25

Things They Don't Teach You in School

"It is costly wisdom that is bought by experience."
— Roger Ascham, English scholar, 1515-1568

I hardly slept. I tossed and turned constantly. I checked my alarm clock almost every hour to see if it was time to get up. I was very nervous. Questions raced through my head. *Can I do this? What do I say to start the meeting? How will he respond? Why do I feel so horrible about this? Am I about to get sick?* Finally, I just got up. It was 4:30 a.m. I got ready and headed to the hospital early. I skipped breakfast. I couldn't eat. I dreaded this day but now it was here.

The meeting was scheduled for mid-morning. I had never had a meeting like this before. I was about to utter a sentence to an employee that I had never said before. *Maybe I should give him one more chance?*

I was twenty-six years old and had recently completed my master's degree. I was now armed with a whopping two years of

115

work experience as a CPA and an MBA diploma. Inwardly, my confidence was a little rattled. I was a rookie hospital administrator. I had only been an assistant administrator for a few months. I was flying by the seat of my pants. *Does anyone know that I have no idea what I'm doing?*

It was time. The department director and a member of her team were sitting in the waiting area. I asked both of them to join me in my office. The director and I had met the day before without this employee to discuss how the meeting would flow. We all sat down at the table in my office.

Though my hands were shaking a bit, I got right to the point. This was not a time to shoot the breeze. Plus, I'm not that good at small talk when I have something important on my mind. *It's time, Jeff—get to the point.*

After providing several examples of this employee's ongoing poor work performance, I said what I had been dreading to say: "Based on your actions that I just outlined, you're fired." No need for discussion. I thanked him for his service and concluded the meeting.

Although it was painful, I was so relieved when it was over. I felt like a huge boulder had been lifted off my shoulders. I took deep breaths. My heart rate was coming down. Although I didn't like delivering that type of information, I knew it was the right thing to do, as well as the best decision for our team. He really fired himself for his actions; I just had to deliver the news.

I still had one unanswered question hovering in my head: *How come no one, in all the classes I took in school, ever taught me how to do this or what to say?*

But Wait, There's More

While writing this chapter, I began to list examples of things they don't teach you in school about what to expect as a leader. The list kept getting longer. In fact, I'm convinced that I could probably write a whole book on this subject alone. Please don't get me wrong, textbooks and theory are important and helpful. However, actual experience leads to far greater and deeper learning. As someone once said, "Until you've been there, you have no idea." This statement is spot on and so true.

I gained valuable knowledge through trial and error on many occasions. It was the actual experience that led to deeper learning and growth. It wasn't from a college class I attended, nor from an article I read. It wasn't from an entertaining and articulate professional speaker who delivered a dazzling presentation, complete with light show and film clips. Sadly, most keynote speakers have never felt the penetrating pressures and challenges of being a leader because they haven't been one. It was just pure theory delivered in a form of entertainment. There were no "bits of gold" to help me become a better leader.

Experience is the master teacher. Here are a few more things I learned through experience that were never taught to me in school:

1. **If you're into popularity, then being a leader might not be your thing.** Many people have the misconception that leaders are admired and beloved by those they lead. This just isn't true. Leaders can be admired, yet disliked. Plus, not everyone is going to like you for whatever reason. They may have never met you but they just don't like you because you're

the leader. They simply don't like who's in charge. Not everyone will appreciate your decisions. You have to learn to take the criticism that comes your way, whether justified or not. It just comes with the territory.

2. **Always have a plan.** When things are trending up, have a plan for how to keep it going. When things are trending down, have a plan for how to turn things around. Have a plan in your back pocket before anyone asks you for a plan. Just as importantly, be able to effectively articulate your plan to others.

3. **Tasmanian devils exist within the organization.** Like it or not, a small number of employees that I like to call Tasmanian devils are just not nice people. They couldn't care less about their teammates, customers, or their company. They are totally disengaged. In fact, the only joy they get is to complain and make things difficult for others. The weird thing is that they don't leave. They would rather stay, be miserable, and make everyone else miserable. It makes no sense to me, but these folks exist. You have to find them, and then jettison them off the team.

4. **Be a boss, not a buddy.** Too many leaders make the mistake of trying to be close friends with those they manage. Their need to be liked blurs their objectivity. It creates multiple problems within the team. It's a rookie mistake that happens way too often, even with experienced leaders. It's true that "it's lonely at the top" at times.

5. **Learn to read the tea leaves.** Develop relationships with your peers and others within the company in order to never get caught off guard by unexpected change. Anticipate when something doesn't seem

right, and seek to clarify. No one likes a busybody, so don't let curiosity contribute to poor performance. However, learn to anticipate what hasn't been said.

Order Now and Receive a Second One Free

So what can you do? As a leader, gladly share with others what you have learned from your experiences. This could include members of your team, your boss, your peers, or those you mentor. Arm them with tools and advice to help them succeed. It's a powerful way to give back. Plus, the intrinsic value it provides you is priceless.

I've gotten more wrinkles and gray hair over the years due to the pressures and challenges of leading. There are countless examples of things I learned from experience that were neither taught to me in school nor presented at a workshop. I'm sure that you have examples, too. Life constantly generates new and complex challenges. You just have to experience them, learn from them, and then pass along that knowledge to others. Great leaders share their "bits of gold" with other leaders striving to learn and grow. Remember, life is about helping others. Learn and pass it on.

Now, what about you?

1. What's the best leadership lesson you have learned through experience that you can pass along to others?
2. How can your work experience help you become a better mentor?

Creating a Legacy of Leadership

"A truly great boss is hard to find,
difficult to leave, and impossible to forget."
— Brigette Hyacinth, author and keynote speaker

I had just finished making hospital rounds early one morning in July 1997 when I learned that our corporate office had scheduled a conference call at 10:00 a.m. Rumors had been swirling for a couple of weeks that a change in leadership at Columbia/HCA was imminent and that an announcement was forthcoming at any moment. I wondered if this was it. In my mind, I prayed that this was the call my colleagues and I had been hoping and waiting for. My heart began beating a little faster with anticipation.

It had been an extremely challenging couple of years, filled with unbelievable pressures and atmospheric expectations by the new company leaders. HCA had merged with Columbia Healthcare in 1994. However, the senior leaders of the new company, Columbia/HCA, would be those from Columbia Healthcare. For those of us from HCA, we felt like we no longer had a voice within the new company. No one was happy.

The terrific culture that Dr. Thomas Frist Jr. and his father had built at HCA was gone. Sadly, the existing leaders from Columbia Healthcare had led us to a place where employee morale was horrific. Turnover was extremely high. Rumor had it that 48 percent of all hospital CEO positions had turned over within the past two years. I was one of the lucky ones who had survived—so far. There was no trust within the organization. Fear reigned. Operational results were stagnant. On top of all that, the FBI had launched an investigation into possible fraudulent activity by some of our senior corporate leaders. It felt as if our company was about to implode. *Please let this be the call announcing that Dr. Frist is coming back.*

The conference call began. I heard a familiar voice come over the speaker. It was Dr. Frist. *Yes! Change is about to occur!* He calmly communicated that a leadership change had been made. He would now move back into the role of president on a short-term basis, and he was bringing back Jack Bovender to be his right-hand person. Jack had been a very successful HCA executive in the past. Dr. Frist outlined his plan for change. It was one of the happiest days in my career. I respected Dr. Frist and had faith that he would lead us out of this abyss.

Dr. Frist had developed a culture of trust and respect over the years. Employees had a voice within the company—our opinions and feedback were welcomed and encouraged. He had carefully developed and nurtured that "family" culture that is so elusive to most organizations. He had vision and a track record of success.

He effectively turned around a sinking ship. He navigated

through the daunting obstacles that confronted us during the shakiest time in our company's history. He rebuilt the foundation, then passed along the leadership to those he trusted to continue the success. His outstanding legacy of leadership will be remembered forever.

The Importance of Legacy

Leaving a great legacy might be the most powerful accomplishment in a leader's career. Let that sink in. Legacy influences the future of the organization even after you are gone. It's a key driver to optimizing your impact on the company and those you led. It's the gift you give while in leadership, and the one you leave when you depart.

I once heard a public speaker tell the audience that leaders begin to think about their legacy around fifty-three years of age. I thought about that statement for a bit. *Surely, that can't be right. You're telling me that leaders don't start thinking about their legacy until they're in their fifties? If that's true, then they've missed it—big time!*

Great leaders realize that their legacy of leadership is what they do today and every single day that they lead. Employees are forming their opinions about them today, not waiting years to determine how they will remember their leader. The most influential leaders—the ones who understand and believe this concept—leave incredible, long-lasting legacies for those they encounter along their leadership journey.

Actions of Legacy-driven Leaders

Legacy-driven leaders focus on making a positive, lasting impact for years to come. Their actions speak louder than their words. Leaders who understand this do the following:

1. **They live a life of high moral character.** People follow leaders they respect. Living a life of honesty, integrity, and service inspires others to follow.
2. **They treat all members of their team equally.** Everyone is equal in God's eyes. Legacy-driven leaders believe this with all their heart. They treat everyone on the team equally and with respect, dignity, and gratitude.
3. **They make tough decisions focused on long-term success.** All too often, some leaders make short-term decisions that are near-sighted and harmful to the organization. Legacy-driven leaders make decisions that support the long-term vision of the company.
4. **They lead with confidence.** They believe in their team and themselves. It shows in their actions, how they conduct themselves around others, and in their decision-making.
5. **They consistently exceed job expectations.** Whether they lead teams to improve quality, increase efficiency, hire top talent, or meet certain financial expectations, legacy-driven leaders consistently find ways to win year after year. They're not one-hit wonders.
6. **They leave the organization in better shape than when they started.** Legacy-driven leaders are judged on their body of work while in the leader's chair. They yearn to make the company better, and they measure their success based on the progress the organization made under their leadership.

Reflecting on Your Legacy

How do you want to be remembered? A leader who cared about their team or a leader who cared more about themselves? A leader who improved their area of responsibility or a leader who simply maintained the status quo?

One of the greatest compliments a leader can receive is to hear positive comments about their effectiveness and influence long after they are gone. Even more importantly, positioning the organization for future success is such a blessing for staff and customers. It's the right thing to do.

New employees who didn't personally know the former leader may join the team, but great leaders are not forgotten. Even though a former leader slowly loses their connection to their former company, their influence on the organization's culture and future success lasts for years to come. It is truly "the gift that keeps on giving."

Now, what about you?

1. How do you want to be remembered as a leader?
2. What are you doing today to positively impact your legacy?

Acknowledgements

One cannot make the journey of life alone. We need others in our lives to celebrate the good times and to navigate the challenging ones.

Serving as a leader is no different. Success is never achieved alone. It takes the help and commitment from others to reach any goal. A leader is just a member of the team. In fact, a leader is nothing without others. Great leaders realize this early in their careers.

There are so many people who helped me along my leadership journey that I need to thank. I'm sure I'll miss several, so please extend a little grace if I do. At the risk of sounding like someone who won an Oscar, Grammy, or CMA Award, I am compelled to acknowledge some key people who have influenced and helped me.

My sincere appreciation to Charles Frasier, my accounting teacher, hero, and mentor while at Lipscomb University. Nothing like a fun conversation about debits and credits!

Thank you to David Solomon for being a great leader and mentor during my first job out of college at KPMG. I was such a newbie and had no clue. Thank you to Larry Burkhart, who helped me get a job with HCA when I was thirty years old. It changed my life. I will always owe you, my friend.

Thank you to Paul Rutledge for hiring me and relocating me to Nashville. You remain a favorite of Jennifer and our girls. I learned so much about great leadership from you. Plus, you are the only boss with whom I prayed—that meant a lot.

My sincere thanks to Steve Corbeil, my last boss before I retired from HCA, who led our team of hospitals to such a high level of success. I was part of a terrific group of hospital CEOs. It was an unbelievable five-year ride, and your leadership made it happen.

Thank you to my friend Louis Joseph of HCA. You know how to win but you always give credit to others. You gave me some great advice on how to improve my presentation skills. A special thanks to Bill Rutherford of HCA for serving as a mentor when it came to career advice. Thank you for recommending that I give back by serving as an executive coach after I retired. I took your advice and I love what I'm doing.

Thank you to Dr. Thomas Frist Jr. for helping start and leading HCA for so many years. I am honored to have worked with such a great company for twenty-five years. Thank you to Jack Bovender, Richard Bracken, Milton Johnson, and Sam Hazen for serving as outstanding presidents of HCA during my time as a hospital CEO. It was an honor to work under your great leadership.

From the bottom of my heart, I thank all the hospital employees and medical staff with whom I had the pleasure of working. Each hospital leadership team was unique and awesome in its own way. Helping others was our mission, and you did it. You lived our values. A very special thank you to the team at TriStar Summit Medical Center. God provided me the opportunity to serve with you. My fourteen years at Summit far exceeded my expectations. Funny how times you love fly by so fast. It was an absolute honor to serve as your CEO.

To all the hospital CEOs with whom I had the pleasure of working, I thank you. I became a better leader by watching and learning from you. The camaraderie and friendships we developed are everlasting.

Many thanks to Epiphany Creative Services, including Jonathan Gullery, Matthew Skar, Patrick Copeland, Stephanie Huffman, and Heather Ebert, my editor, for helping me bring this book to life.

And most importantly, to my family. Thank you to my late mother and father for providing a loving home, teaching me right from wrong, paying for my education, and putting Christ first in your lives. Thank you to Tim and Marilyn Gentry, my parents-in-law, for treating me as if I were your own son. I learned so much from Tim, who passed away in 1998, about the Bible, metal detecting, and investing.

Thank you to Jennifer, my lovely wife of thirty-six years and counting, for being by my side the whole way. Your love, encouragement, and support means so much. Plus, relocating seven times was a lot to ask but you did it. Thank you for saying "I do" in 1985. My love and gratitude to our daughters, Ashleigh and Emily. You are a true blessing from God for which I'm forever thankful. I am very proud of both of you.

About the Author

Jeff Whitehorn, LFACHE, ACC, is an author, speaker, and executive coach certified by the global accrediting body International Coaching Federation (ICF). After earning his Bachelor of Science from Lipscomb University and his MBA from the University of Alabama, Jeff spent twenty-nine years as a healthcare executive, serving twenty-five of those as a hospital CEO. He founded Whitehorn Coaching & Consulting LLC after his retirement from HCA Healthcare. Jeff continues to serve in leadership roles as a member of community boards and within his church. He and his wife, Jennifer, reside in Brentwood, Tennessee. They have two grown daughters, Ashleigh and Emily.

NOTES